The Classic Boat

The Classic Boat

By the Editors of
TIME-LIFE BOOKS

The
TIME-LIFE Library of Boating

TIME-LIFE BOOKS, ALEXANDRIA, VIRGINIA

The TIME-LIFE Library of Boating

Editorial Staff for The Classic Boat:
Editor: George Constable
Assistant Editor: Bryce S. Walker
Text Editors: Wendy Buehr Murphy, Harvey B. Loomis
Picture Editor: Nancy Shuker
Designer: James Eisenman
Associate Designers: Ed Frank, Marion Flynn Logan
Staff Writers: Jane Colihan, Stuart Gannes,
John von Hartz, Kate Slate
Chief Researchers: Elizabeth D. Meyer, Wendy A. Rieder
Researchers: Charles Blackwell, Reese Hassig,
Helen M. Hinkle, Catherine Ireys, Mary K. Moran Jaroff
Design Assistants: Rosi Cassano, Joan Hoffman,
Anne McCormick

Editorial Production
Production Editor: Douglas B. Graham
Operations Manager: Gennaro C. Esposito
Assistant Production Editor: Feliciano Madrid
Quality Control: Robert L. Young (director),
James J. Cox (assistant), Michael G. Wight (associate)
Art Coordinator: Anne B. Landry
Copy Staff: Susan B. Galloway (chief),
Kathleen Beakley, Mary Ellen Slate, Pearl Sverdlin,
Florence Keith, Celia Beattie
Picture Department: Dolores A. Littles, Zenona Green

The Cover: Sending forth a great cloud of white vapor and a whistle, *Mt. Rattlesnake* glides across an inlet on Lake Winnipesaukee in New Hampshire at a languorous three knots. The steam yacht, built at the turn of the century and lovingly maintained ever since, was participating in an antique-boat regatta, one of many invitationals held annually in the United States as part of the steadily increasing classic-boat revival.

The Consultants: John D. Atkin, who is a yacht designer and professional surveyor, has written numerous articles for boating magazines. He is a member of both the Society of Naval Architects and Marine Engineers and the National Association of Marine Surveyors.

William A. Baker is a naval architect and is Curator of the Francis Russell Hart Nautical Museum at the Massachusetts Institute of Technology. He is also the author of a number of books and articles on classic boats.

Halsey Herreshoff, a noted racing sailor and marine architect, has been building and refurbishing both powerboats and sailing craft for 25 years. A designer of custom and manufactured yachts, he owns his own boatyard, belongs to the Society of Naval Architects and Marine Engineers, and has published articles in most of the major boating periodicals.

Rob Pittaway, a naval architect and research associate at Mystic Seaport, has rebuilt several small classic wooden boats and has designed rowing and sailing craft. He has also written articles for the major boating publications.

Correspondents: Elisabeth Kraemer (Bonn); Margot Hapgood, Dorothy Bacon (London); Susan Jonas, Lucy T. Voulgaris (New York); Maria Vincenza Aloisi, Josephine du Brusle (Paris); Ann Natanson (Rome). Valuable assistance was also provided by Carolyn T. Chubet, Miriam Hsia (New York).

Contents

The Renascence of Classic Watercraft

The Renascence of Classic Watercraft

by John Gardner

Snowflakes were flying one winter's evening when the *Lizzie M.* slipped into Rockland Harbor north of Portland, Maine, just ahead of a northeaster. Aboard was fisherman Tommy Martelock with a fresh catch of haddock. Local buyers refused to give him the price he wanted, so Tommy said he'd run his catch to Portland. "You'll never make it, not tonight!" they scoffed. Said Tommy: "Like hell I won't!" and set sail. All that black, howling night he pounded south through the squalls and freezing scud, fetched Portland at sunup, and got his price. That is how the Friendship sloop *Lizzie M.* earned her reputation as one of the ablest vessels on the Maine coast.

Just under 40 feet and as handsome and sweetly lined as any yacht, the *Lizzie M.* carried a 32-foot boom, a 22-foot gaff and 975 square feet of canvas in her mainsail alone. She was one of the sloop-bowed Friendships designed and built by Charles Morse at Thomaston, Maine, in 1917. That was during the twilight years of the working Friendships, though; working sail was giving way to new types of engine-powered craft. In 1926, following Martelock's death, the *Lizzie M.* was converted to a yacht—to the delight of her new owner, G. K. Briggs of Essex, Connecticut. "She was an exceptionally smart sailer," he recalled years later, "fast to windward in a blow, with an unusual ability to keep moving through a chop in light airs. She was easy to reef down. Under two reefs and the jumbo [forestaysail], she balanced beautifully and could carry through any summer westerly. In short, she was a vessel."

And, in short, the *Lizzie M.* epitomized the classic boat—functional, able, an authentic and satisfying survivor of earlier times. These days, growing numbers of boats like the *Lizzie M.* can be seen swinging gracefully to their moorings in anchorages all around the United States. There are beamy catboats, elegant old launches, sturdy gaff-rigged ketches, venerable power cruisers, sleek pulling boats and trim sailing dories. Some are cherished antiques, some are reproductions made of wood or even of shiny fiberglass. All attest to the fact that, as with so many other examples of early American ingenuity, the classic boat is having an enormous popular revival.

Although there are many aspects of this renascence, I think it is fair to say that most classic boats have histories as workboats. The Friendship sloop had many builders—four of them Morse brothers—but most were fishermen and they designed their Friendships primarily for utility rather than recreation.

Throughout the 19th Century, in unnumbered small boatyards, in sheds and lean-tos on coast, lakeshore and riverfront, other working boats were being built by the thousands. Dories for the Grand Banks, whale boats for the Arctic and South seas, log canoes for oystermen, bugeyes and brogans, pungies, pinkies and skiffs were being turned out, mostly by individuals who were as handy with the adze as with hand lines, traps and oyster tongs.

Some of these boats were as versatile as they were functional. The graceful pulling boat called a Whitehall, for example, was used by New York Harbor pilots, newspaper reporters and ship chandlers, and by Battery boatmen as a water taxi. It was also a favorite of the "crimps," who kidnapped sailors on the waterfront and delivered them to ships needing crews. Beyond being a classic rowing boat, the Whitehall also adapted well to sail, and was used under her small sailing rig for longer distances, especially around Boston and San Francisco harbors, and, on the Sacramento River, for fishing.

By and large, the working craft were also beautiful. Their designs were the natural result of a vigorous process of functional·selection, and the efficient line of hull and practical arrangement of mast or oars also usually happened to be graceful and attractive. Furthermore, although the boatbuilders may not have thought of their work as an art form, many of them unquestionably had a discerning eye for beauty.

Take the Adirondack guide boat. Devised and perfected by North Woods

Author John Gardner sets brace and bit to the floor of a Whitehall under construction in one of the workshops at Connecticut's Mystic Seaport. Associate Curator for small-craft studies there, Gardner includes among his many activities the supervising of the Small Craft Boatshop where Seaport boatbuilders construct reproductions of classic wood boats and restore old ones for the museum's growing collection.

guides, it is a marvel of lightness and strength, as artfully constructed as a violin, yet enduring enough to last over a lifetime of strenuous use. For half a century this exquisite rowing boat provided the primary means of transportation throughout hundreds of miles of northern wilderness. Because the waterways were broken with rapids that necessitated long portages over rough terrain, the guide boat's builders pared down its weight, literally shaving by shaving, until they had perfected a 16-foot craft—fully equipped with seats, backrest, oars and paddle—that weighed only 72 pounds. In the process it became something more than a mere conveyance: an Adirondack guide boat was exhibited at the 1967 Montreal Expo as an example of American folk art.

The independent craftsmen who turned out such works of art were greatly admired in their communities, and the best of them were often remembered for generations. They stubbornly guarded their standards, working under the eyes of their peers, all of whom were highly critical of bad workmanship. Their dedication was exemplified by Gil Smith of Long Island, New York, who set up his yard in Patchogue in 1876 and designed and built nearly 400 of his famous Great South Bay catboats. His wife sewed the sails, and often a finished boat was sailed to its new home port by Gil, his wife and his daughter, dressed up for the occasion.

Even while small craft did the work of a busy maritime nation, they, as well as larger boats, were also providing fun and sport. Recreational boating in America really started to grow in the mid-19th Century. The New York Yacht Club was organized in 1844; it was in 1851 that George Steer's schooner, the yacht *America*, modeled on the New York Harbor pilot boat, sailed to England and won the historic race that led to the world's most famous yachting competition: the America's Cup Race.

More and more amateur boatmen turned for pleasure craft to the professional builders of workboats. The classic Swampscott dory, originally designed for fishing off the New England coast, was adapted to daysailing, and by 1910 these leg-of-mutton-rigged dories were not only one of the most popular pleasure craft on the Northeastern seaboard, their popularity had even extended to the Great Lakes.

The proliferation of small craft for pleasure also included all sorts of rowing boats. By 1870 there were 237 rowing clubs in the Northeastern United States and neighboring Canadian provinces, with 11,000 members. Whitehalls and guide boats and Saint Lawrence skiffs became common weekend craft. With the vast increase in the popularity of hunting and lake fishing for recreation, all manner of rowing boats dotted American lakes.

Then, with the introduction of the gasoline engine, the popularity of small sailing and rowing boats suffered a severe blow. Bulky steam and naphtha engines had already been used on launches, but when the lighter and more compact gasoline engine appeared in the United States in 1878, the days of the working sailboat and rowing boat were numbered. Before too long, few fishermen bothered to row much; lobstermen now used boats with motors, and the Maine guide who once rowed all day now relaxed in his "putt-putt" as it sped easily, if noisily, across the water. The old workboats were left rotting on the beach. When, in 1964, a group attempted to build a model of a classic Beachcomber-Alpha sailing dory for the Peabody Museum in Salem, Massachusetts, not a single surviving example of this boat could be found. Fortunately, they were able to obtain the lines and some old photographs from the daughter of an original builder.

Yet it turned out that classic boats, though endangered species, had not disappeared altogether. Little by little, they were rescued from extinction, as more Americans realized that these traditional watercraft deserved to be cherished and preserved. The revival was further stimulated by Howard I. Chapelle in the 1930s with a series of pioneering articles on classic workboats for *Yachting* magazine. Then, in 1941, he wrote *Boatbuilding*, followed 10 years later by *American Small Sailing Craft*. Both volumes continue to be primary references for all those interested in reviving vintage craft. With his enthusiasm for these boats, and his elegant drawings of their plans, Chapelle did more than any other American to rescue the classic boat.

Meanwhile, during the 1940s, the famous yacht designer, L. Francis Herreshoff, wrote a series of illustrated articles for *Rudder* magazine on the construction of various boats, following many classic techniques. Some of the articles were then republished in book form, under the title *The Common Sense of Yacht Design,* and were of great influence in the revival of classic craft. Beginning in the 1950s, a few museums stirred even more interest in classic boats by searching out and restoring forgotten and abandoned examples of them. The Adirondack Museum at Blue Mountain Lake, New York, opened in 1957, with a small collection of workboats indigenous to the Adirondack region, particularly the famous guide boat. The museum's collection came to number more than 150 boats housed in a temperature- and humidity-controlled building.

The museum at Mystic, Connecticut, which formerly concentrated on the history of large sailing ships, added 54 small classic boats to its exhibits between 1950 and 1960. With continued steady growth, it eventually boasted the largest number of small craft in any North American museum, some 250.

The museum's exhibits of restored classic craft continue to stimulate the interest of many. But an equally significant factor is the changing attitude of people themselves. Reacting against the uniformity and extravagant styling of mass production, they turn in increasing numbers to classic watercraft for the opportunity these boats afford to express individual choice and creativity. While hard statistics are scant, the evidence is everywhere. In 1961, just to take an example, the Friendship Sloop Society was founded by Bernard Mackenzie and a small group of owners of surviving sloops, who gathered at Friendship, Maine, for what they called their first homecoming. Fifteen years later there were nearly 300 members and 179 sloops; 52 of them sailed in the annual three-day Friendship Sloop Regatta.

The catboat, too, has made a dramatic recovery. Originally a working craft for fishing and transportation in the coastal waters from Cape Cod to southern New Jersey, this shallow-draft, wide-bodied, jibless sailboat was also highly popular with recreational sailors at the turn of the century. Then it, too, seemed bound for oblivion as sailors spurned the homey craft in favor of sleeker, more up-to-date designs. But in 1962, 49 catboat owners held a rendezvous at Duck Island, off the Connecticut shore of Long Island Sound, to form a Catboat Association. Within about 15 years membership had grown to 707, of whom 544 had acquired or built their own catboats.

The first antique boat show in the United States was held in Clayton, New York, in 1963, when a few summer residents in the Thousand Islands area at the headwaters of the Saint Lawrence River got together to celebrate the restoration of a battered old motor launch. Each summer since the whole town of Clayton has been involved, and the event has grown to a two-day affair. Visitors come from as far away as Florida, and in one recent year more than 100 classic boats were on display, some of them more than 75 years old.

Similar rendezvous and shows have taken place in Maine, Rhode Island, Connecticut, California, Washington and Ottawa. The classic boat will never replace the easily maintained fiberglass sailboat for many racing sailors and those who have neither the time nor inclination to mess about building or restoring their craft; but the trend is unmistakable: the classic workboat as a pleasure boat is making an impressive comeback among those who delight as much in the boat itself as in getting out on the water.

There are at least three ways a boat lover can join this select but growing circle. The easiest, of course, is to buy a reproduction. Some classic designs have become so popular that copies of them are turned out in commercial quantities. Most of these imitations are made of fiberglass, thus they combine the classic lines and sailing or rowing qualities with modern ease of maintenance. Some have also been adapted to the present yachtsman's ideas of comfort. Many of the early catboats, for example, while comfortably beamy, had precious little headroom below; some of the modern copies have been modified to provide standing headroom.

Perhaps the most rewarding way of acquiring a classic boat, however, is to find an old one and restore it. This is difficult but not impossible. Antique boats can still be found, if one knows where to look and—just as important —what to look for. In remote gunk holes and along urban waterfronts, in far corners of boatyards, in dilapidated sheds, venerable barns and run-down boathouses, abandoned classics are yet to be found. Most of them are in disrepair, but some are in surprisingly good condition—a tribute in part to the durability that was built into them.

The most famous example of classic restoration is *Spray*, the ancient 37-foot fishing sloop that Captain Joshua Slocum found in 1892 rotting in a field in Fairhaven, Massachusetts. He rebuilt her and single-handedly sailed 46,000 miles around the world. Slocum has been an inspiration to thousands of classic-boat enthusiasts; many *Sprays* have been built in respectful imitation of the original, and some have been sailed in her wake.

Just as satisfying as restoring a classic boat is building one from the keel up. All the patience, perseverance and sweat involved is richly compensated for in the reward that comes when the boat you have constructed with your own hands is at last launched upon the waters.

How well I remember the first boat I built—or, rather, helped my father build: a skiff to use on our river at the head of Maine's Passamaquoddy Bay. It was fashioned from cedar and oak that we had cut the winter before and had hauled over the snow to the sawmill. That was 60 years ago, and the thrill remains. Since then I have built or worked on other skiffs, as well as dories, peapods, launches, lobster boats, draggers, yachts for power and sail, on historic restorations and on reproductions. Every one of them was a deeply gratifying as well as a fascinating adventure. I am still building boats, with the same pleasure that the first one gave me.

Hundreds of other Americans are learning to find the same rewards in boatshops and museums all around the country where, in recent years, training courses have gotten under way. Mystic Seaport in Connecticut holds a small-craft workshop for a weekend in June and also rents out a movie on dory building, as well as selling at low cost the lines and details of many of the classic craft in its collection. The Bath Marine Museum's Apprenticeshop in Bath, Maine, has both apprentice and restoration programs for small craft. The Adirondack Museum will supply plans for the famous guide boat. At Strawbery Banke, a historic preservation site in old Portsmouth, New Hampshire, a program that builds classic dories and other small craft for sale, also offers apprenticeships for those interested in learning to make them.

The spectacle of so many people returning to the classic boats—building or restoring them, buying or simply admiring them—is gratifying but perhaps not surprising. In a way, it is part of the trend back to simpler, saner, more natural ways of living. This feeling was expressed by a young settler on Waldron Island, in the state of Washington, who built, of native lumber and mostly with hand tools, a 17-foot Whitehall.

"I feel this Whitehall fits into the natural beauty of the San Juan Islands here in Puget Sound," he writes. "It is not possible fully to appreciate the serenity of the area with an engine roaring and the smell of gasoline fumes. Besides, the combination of oar and sail feels so much more dependable than an engine. And that's what I wanted, a combination boat, one that would row swiftly when the wind dies, which happens frequently here in the summer, and sail well. I plan to use it for transportation to the various islands, as well as for pleasure."

So in Puget Sound anyway, the classic workboat may have come full circle, being used for transportation as well as simply for recreation. In other areas these former workboats may work again. But most of them will be used for pleasure. And for those who appreciate the heritage, the seaworthiness and the graceful beauty of the classic boat, it is pleasure compounded.

1 The world of classic boats encompasses an astonishing variety of craft of all sorts and sizes, propelled by every imaginable source of power. There are elegantly curved Whitehall pulling boats, boxy gunning skiffs with a handkerchief of sail, broad-bellied catboats like the vessel at left, pencil-thin gasoline runabouts and roly-poly steam launches seemingly powered by a mixture of wood, smoke and determination. All of these differences are explained by the one characteristic that these craft have in common: each of them has a particular ability to perform the job it was designed to do.

The coast of New England produced a large assortment of fishing boats,

TRADITIONAL BOATS ON PARADE

with differing hull shapes that evolved to meet the individual needs of each locality. The Maine peapod, ancestor of the fiberglass reproduction shown on page 33, was a rowing and sailing craft used to retrieve lobster pots. Because the lobstermen needed to put one foot on the gunwale and lean over the side to haul the pots aboard, Maine boatbuilders gave the peapod full, round bilges and extra weight for maximum stability.

There were half a dozen or more specialized kinds of dories, which fishermen rowed out in all weather to hand-line for cod, mackerel or other ocean fish. Others were lighter and trimmer than the Maine peapod, like the Swampscott dory (page 16). All of these ocean-going workboats had flared sides so that they grew beamier—and thus more stable—as they settled deeper into the water with their catch of fish.

Classic rigs were as varied as classic hull designs—and they also were devised with a purpose. For the loose-footed spritsail on the North Jersey beach skiff on page 19, this purpose was ease of handling and efficiency. The unstayed mast was easy to set up with no wasted motion, and without a boom to constrict the foot the sail automatically assumed its proper aerodynamic shape. However, a Gloucester schooner had a more elaborate rig, designed for speed; the captain aboard the fisherman prototype of the schooner on page 26 could race home with his catch under as many as six different flights of canvas, weather permitting.

Speed also was a prime consideration in the design of most early powerboats—though today no one in a hurry would jump aboard one of the tubby antique steam launches pictured on pages 20-21. They are relics from the pioneer days of marine power, when each one had to wait about half an hour before its massive boiler built up enough pressure just to get moving. As gasoline engines replaced steam, power plants became lighter, more compact, more convenient—and much easier to start. At the same time, the hulls that held them became leaner, longer and faster; by 1906 there were slender runabouts that skimmed over the water at up to 18 knots. But many vintage power craft were designed with another purpose in mind, no less compelling than the urge to get places quickly. This was the simple desire of their owners to show off, which expressed itself in a conspicuous elegance of design and construction. A boat such as the custom cruiser on pages 28-29 might have a varnished mahogany hull and paneling, leather upholstery and a king's ransom in gleaming brass fittings. One builder that epitomized this sense of quality and style —and the careful workmanship that went into all the classic boats on the following pages—was the Electric Boat Company of Bayonne, New Jersey. For 55 years, Elco turned out everything from small electric launches, some of which are shown on page 14, to luxury cruisers. Then, in 1948, when the best materials were becoming both scarce and expensive, the firm advertised that it was going out of business. The directors decided that if they could no longer build classics, they would simply quit building them.

A 26-foot gaff-rigged catboat, built in 1894, waits out a calm on Barnegat Bay. Restored in 1938, she has a wide, shallow-draft hull typical of the East Coast shoal-water craft of her time.

Launches and Putt-Putts

A 15-foot Adirondack skiff powered by an antique Elto outboard putters across Lake George in New York. The first Adirondack skiffs were double-enders, built for rowing; this one, turned out during the 1920s, was given a square stern with an engine mount for auxiliary power. Her present owner bought the boat and engine together in 1975, after the skiff had been in a garage for 10 years. He replaced two seats, gave her a fresh coat of paint—and started the dusty 1.8-horsepower engine on the first try.

Soundless electric boats, like this 12-foot launch built in the 1930s by the Electric Boat Company, are the only power-driven craft permitted on the private Tuxedo Park Lake in New York State. The engine runs on two 6-volt automotive-type batteries and can propel the boat in calm waters at about four knots.

*A 1901 Lozier launch leaves almost no wake as she chugs through
Lake Winnipesaukee in New Hampshire. The Lozier Motor Company
was a producer of early automobiles; the firm began building marine
hulls and engines at the turn of the century, when gasoline engines
entered the market. According to the launch's owner, who bought the
launch in the mid-1950s, refinished the hull and replaced the
engine, she may be the only Lozier that is still floating.*

Pulling Boats

This collection of docked pulling boats includes a Whitehall (bottom), two Swampscott dories (center) and a skiff (top). Each was designed primarily for rowing —though two shown here carry masts—and each has characteristics in common with the others. Compared to modern boats, all four are fairly heavily constructed, so that once underway they maintain momentum. And all are relatively long (12 to 16 feet), which helps them stay on course even if the rower pulls harder on one oar than on the other.

The double-ended lapstrake Canadian craft at left has oars that have curved blades to provide a better bite in the water. The owner discovered the boat on a farm located near Rockport, Ontario, and he believes that she was built some time around 1920.

This copy of a Banks dory is specially designed to perform as well under sail as when rowed. To counteract the tendency to heel, she is beamier than standard rowing dories, like those above left, and her sides have more pronounced curves. Her sail is Dacron, dyed to resemble old canvas sails treated with oak-bark preservative.

Beachboats and Skiffs

The cat-ketch Glory Anna II, shown above sailing off Mystic, Connecticut, is a replica of a Block Island cowhorn, a design named for the hull's crescent-shaped profile. In the 1800s, cowhorns were used extensively for hand-line fishing around the coastal islands of Rhode Island. Their double-ended design enabled them to reach shore even with waves breaking behind them. After jetties were built, better protecting the harbors, cowhorns began dying out. To keep the type from disappearing, a Rhode Island boat designer built Glory Anna II in 1948, using plans drawn up from old photographs and sketches.

A gaff-rigged Barnegat Bay sneakbox, a beefed-up pleasure-boating version of an early 1800s gunning skiff, sails before the wind off Westport, Connecticut. Both its name and its basic shape evolved from the so-called sinkbox, a rectangular, flat-bottomed hunter's craft that rode low in the water and acted as a stationary blind and as a stalking vehicle for sneaking up on ducks.

Right Arm, a modern copy of a North Jersey beach skiff, lies moored at a Connecticut dock, with a hand-crafted manila fender over the side for protection. A hundred years ago and more, ancestors of this skiff were used for fishing the New Jersey coast. Because harbors were few, boats had to be launched from the beach, often through rough surf, and beached again at night. Their lapstrake, or clinker, construction was made to withstand the constant friction of being dragged over stony landings. Right Arm carries a spritsail and jib, and can be rowed.

Stylish Steamboats

Leaving trails of vapor behind them, three entries in a Lake George steamboat regatta chug along at a walloping six knots. Steamboats from all over the Northeast compete in the August event. West Coast steam lovers gather at a summer rendezvous on Puget Sound that is sponsored by a group called the Puget Sound Live Steamers.

For classic-boat tinkerers like the top-hatted helmsman of River Queen, no mode of marine propulsion can match the lusty old steam engine for pure style. The Queen, a 23-footer built deep in the water to counterbalance its massive high-rise machinery, is a replica of an early turn-of-the-century launch, and has been fitted with a 100-year-old wood-fired boiler. Starting with a full load of wood (about one third of a cord), the River Queen can cruise for two and a half days.

A Herreshoff steam launch with the unconventional name of Mt. Rattlesnake winds through a leafy inlet. The 22-foot boat was designed and built about 1900 and has had several different steam engines; the present boiler is fired by diesel oil. The owner found the boat in Massachusetts, did some light hull repair, and added a canopy and a steam whistle (hitched alongside the stack).

Working Sailboats

A Bahama sloop scuds along the edge of a storm cloud during the annual Out Island Regatta off Exuma Island. Bahama sloops, from 20 to 40 feet in length, are one of two sail-powered workboat types still plying North American waters. Several hundred of these deep-hulled, broad-transomed craft gather conchs and transport light cargo in the Bahamas, where steady trade winds make sail power practical. The huge, loose-footed mainsail is as long across the bottom as it is along the luff. In place of complicated reefing gear, the sail is rigged with a so-called tricing line, which reduces sail by raising the foot.

Skipjacks are the second of the two motorless boats still active; those above are shown competing in a weekend race on Chesapeake Bay. They manage to stay economically competitive with powerboats in oyster dredging because strict conservation laws permit powerboats to dredge only two days a week, while skipjacks can dredge for seven. About 30 of these broad-beamed, shallow-draft craft, most of them 60 years old or older, are still operating. Each carries a motorized yawl-boat on davits; if the wind dies on a day when power is legal, these boats are lowered into the water and used to push the parent craft.

A 30-foot Jonesport lobster boat christened Laura W speeds toward the finish of the annual Fourth of July race on Maine's Moosabec Reach. The first of these deep-bowed, flat-stern workboats was built sometime in the 1920s; duplicates and variations have continued to be built ever since. Most of the boats have Oldsmobile and Buick automobile engines with special cooling systems to adapt them to marine use. Newer models are fitted with more economical diesel engines. Both types of engine provide a good turn of speed, and over the two-mile race course, a lobster boat can reach about 40 mph.

Powerboats for Work and Fun

Thirty-eight-foot Excalibur, above, is a 1929 mahogany Chris-Craft commuter, a model often used to take businessmen living near New York, Chicago and Detroit to their offices. Many such cruisers —including Excalibur—came equipped with two sets of controls and two windshields, so a chauffeur could go forward and take command of the vessel while the owner and friends relaxed in the cockpit.

A sleek 26-foot Chris-Craft runabout named Jacqueline shows off her double-cockpit design and rare, light mahogany hull. Built in 1930, she was restored to mint condition in 1970, given a new engine—and loaned for the filming of the movie The Great Gatsby.

Traditional Sailing Yachts

Ketch-rigged Tioga surges forward in the Master Mariners Regatta, a classic-boat competition on San Francisco Bay. L. Francis Herreshoff, son of the formidable Nathanael (pages 66-77), drew up the lines for this 57-foot yacht in 1931, and later pronounced her one of his favorite designs. A beamy centerboarder, Tioga is an able and versatile cruising vessel that handles well in any weather. In fact, she is used by charter groups who come aboard to learn classic-boat seamanship—for example, how to make chafe-preventing baggywrinkle (shown here in the rigging) out of frayed Dacron lines.

The 57-foot schooner Yankee, right, was built in 1906 at a yard whose location is now the site of the San Francisco Yacht Club. When the yacht was about to be launched, the famous earthquake shook the city, and Yankee, still in her cradle, overturned. Although superstitious sailors of the day feared the accident might signal the start of an unlucky career, her stout, well-built hull sustained little damage, and Yankee later developed into a successful racer. She is still winning in regattas for classic designs.

Freda, a 32-foot gaff-rigged sloop, gathers speed as the wind freshens on San Francisco Bay. Built in Belvedere, California, in 1885, she is one of the oldest boats on the West Coast, and the only vessel still sailing that was present at the opening of the Corinthian Yacht Club in San Francisco in 1886. When her restorer bought her in 1955, she was in need of extensive hull repair. Working with friends, he replaced her mast and rebuilt over half the above-water hull. He ordered a new suit of Dacron sails and synthetic lines for her; however, he did not convert the lighting system to electricity: Freda's cabin and running lights are still her original kerosene-burning lamps.

A Stately Cruiser

A 1929 power cruiser surges past Angel Island in San Francisco Bay, her plumb bow knifing through the chop. Designed and built by the West Coast firm of Stephens Brothers, the 47-footer is framed and planked with Port Orford cedar—a straight-grained, rot-resistant wood once plentiful in Oregon but now virtually impossible to obtain. The boat's deckhouse and aftercabin are teak: to preserve their lustrous surface, the owner applies fresh varnish every three months.

CAREFREE FIBERGLASS MODELED ON CLASSIC LINES

This comely 32-foot fiberglass reproduction of a New England lobster boat will cruise along at 16 knots under her 160-horsepower diesel engine. Her cockpit can be fitted with an awning, as here, or a flying bridge, and she will sleep up to four passengers.

Over the past decade so many yachtsmen have begun clamoring to own and sail in boats of classic design that commercial boatyards have begun turning out virtually line-perfect reproductions—in fiberglass. There are pinkies, pulling boats, catboats, lobster boats and whaleboats, and scaled-down fishing schooners—all with fiberglass hulls or wood hulls with glass sheathing. A California firm has even come up with a fiberglass copy of an 1890 electric-power launch.

On these vessels, the builders have managed to preserve the distinctive looks and handling qualities of the originals. And the fiberglass construction of the hulls offers many tadvantages that turn-of-the-century sailors would never have thought possible.

The first is strength. When a wooden boat works in a seaway, the timbers tend to twist, and in some key areas, such as the mast step, they lose their strength. Fiberglass is better at withstanding this type of twisting athwartship strain. Furthermore, the one-piece construction of fiberglass hulls eliminates multiple seams between individual planks, and between cabin house and deck—prime sources of leaks on wooden craft. With no need for heavy internal frames and timbers, a glass hull is roomier below.

For most weekend yachtsmen, however, the principal advantage of fiberglass is low maintenance—as any boatowner who spends his summer scraping, caulking and repainting a wooden hull knows. With little more than an annual cleaning, waxing and polishing, a fiberglass hull is ready for the water.

A fiberglass Crotch Island pinky—a 21-foot reproduction of a double-ended Maine fishing boat—skims along Mill Creek, near Annapolis, Maryland.

This 32-foot fiberglass Jonesport lobster boat has the same clean, spare lines as its original wooden counterpart (page 24). Below are lockers that double as bunks; if desired, the cabin can be fitted with a galley, a head and bunks that sleep two to four. A 160-horsepower diesel engine drives her at a top speed of 17 knots, and the spacious, obstruction-free cockpit is well suited to almost any kind of angling. In fact, about half of the fiberglass lobstermen currently built are sold to commercial fishermen, the other half to yachtsmen as pleasure boats.

Trimmed in teak and carrying a Sitka-spruce spar, this fiberglass replica of a Herreshoff 12½ has a club-footed jib and old-fashioned mast hoops to attach the gaff-rigged sail to the mast. Named for its length on the waterline (it is 16 feet overall), the first of these craft was designed by N. G. Herreshoff in 1914. A Massachusetts firm has been building the glass version since 1972.

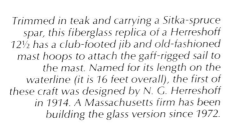

The Cape Cod catboat, used for fishing during the 1800s, today makes a seaworthy day sailer or cruising boat. This beamy 22-foot model, manufactured in Massachusetts, has two berths and a small galley in its enclosed cabin. The mast, supported by a single headstay, is aluminum.

Spritsail furled, a 16-foot fiberglass peapod makes its way under oars. Peapods, which got their name from their upswept double ends, were once popular among lobster fishermen off the Maine coast. A Maine-based builder produces them today for boatmen looking for a small boat that can be easily rowed or sailed. The fiberglass hull is fitted with a Sitka-spruce mast, a mahogany rudder, and mahogany or teak trim.

A 32-foot double-ended Eastport pinky with tanbark-colored Dacron sails tows its tender along the coast of Maine. The original boats of this type were used primarily in Maine's sardine industry; modern replicas make comfortable cruising boats for four. Their hulls are constructed of cedar and then covered with several layers of polypropylene cloth to add strength and to reduce maintenance. For auxiliary power, they have 25-horsepower diesel engines.

This 25-foot schooner-rigged double-ender is a replica of a Tancook Whaler, a design originating at Tancook Island, Nova Scotia, about 1870. The hull is fiberglass, but the deck, thwarts, rub rail, bowsprit and all trim are of wood. For added authenticity, the Dacron sails, not shown here, are cut with the narrow vertical panels commonly found on 19th Century fore-and-afters.

The wineglass transom and basic lines of this Connecticut-built fiberglass rowboat were adapted from one of the best known of all old pulling boats—the Whitehall. Weighing 145 pounds, the boat was deliberately built to be both heavy and long enough to maintain its momentum when it was rowed.

Contemporary Classics

Appreciation for classic lines has grown to such an extent that many of today's designers have begun to turn out neoclassic vessels of their own devising—craft that are not replicas, but that borrow any number of features from older boats. For example, designer Halsey Herreshoff took a catboat's beamy hull shape, a clipper bow, traditional trailboards, a gaff rig and an outboard rudder and blend-

ed them into the *Eagle*, the entirely new design that is shown here. In the days before fiberglass made possible mass production, no such amalgam would have been economically feasible, because the complex curves involved in shaping a clipper bow on a boat this size would be extremely difficult to execute in wood. But with fiberglass, there is virtually no limit, in

terms of construction feasibility, on shape.

By using similar materials and techniques, other marine architects have created miniature tugboats and trawlers, fishing schooners, tubby cat-rigged day sailers, as well as character cruising boats like Stone Horse sloops and Newport ketches—all of which combine the look of antiquity with the convenience of modern fiberglass boats.

The beauty and utility of any classic boat begin with the artful manner in which it was created. During the handcrafting days of boatbuilding, the smallest wherry or sailing dinghy was commonly fitted together with an economy of line and an attention to workmanship that would bankrupt the modern mass producer. A catboat like that at left, for example, might contain some 200 separate pieces of wood, each of which was carefully cut to shape and joined together—a process that sometimes took its builder half a year to complete. Like a piece of signed antique cabinetry, the boat was likely to contain a few idiosyncratic touches of the builder's own—perhaps lathe-turned seat sup-

THE ANATOMY OF A HULL

ports. However, the techniques that were used to bring such a boat into being were shared, often unknowingly, by craftsmen throughout the Western world. And an understanding of these principles adds immeasurably to the pleasure and sense of discovery that today is so much a part of owning, studying or simply working with classic boats.

As the first step in the building of any boat, classic or modern, the boatwright must start with a clear idea of its desired shape. In ancient times this shape existed mainly in the head of the builder as he pounded and lashed his craft together—and for the small, simple American workboats of a few generations ago, this elementary mental image was often enough. However, sometime in the 15th Century, those men who were tasked with the building of larger vessels began by working up scale drawings, and later on they whittled scale models of their hulls. The use of scale models became particularly popular among American designers, such as the celebrated Rhode Islander Nathanael Herreshoff, and the catboat-building Crosby family of Cape Cod, each of whom conceived a new design and then made his concept real by carving out a miniature prototype. These models showed only one side of the hull. Since a boat's shape is symmetrical, the builder would simply double the half model when constructing the full-sized craft.

The alternate method of drafting lines onto paper is the technique generally preferred by today's designers, both for creating new boats and for recording the lines of vintage craft for archives. Essentially, a lines plan represents, in two dimensions, the contour lines of the half model (overleaf). Whichever method the designer used, he would take a series of critical measurements, called offsets, along the contour lines of the hull, which would then serve as a guide to the builder.

Sometimes the designer would also supply the builder with another set of plans (page 44) showing the details of the boat's construction—the shape of its keel, the location of its frames, the type of planking to use, the placement of key strengthening members, and so on. The construction plan generally presented a cutaway profile of the hull and cabin, and one or more cross sections depicting any special parts that needed explaining.

Having the boat's shape clearly in mind and with the construction plan in hand, the boatwright could then start to build. He would begin by creating a plan of his own—a full-sized rendition of the boat's lines on the floor of his boat shed. This so-called lofting of the lines became a pattern for the creation of the templates that were used to cut out the lumber. The subsequent steps that the builder followed in piecing the boat together varied from yard to yard and from boat to boat. Generally, large vessels took shape right side up, supported by a scaffolding, while many smaller craft were put together upside down over a set of molds. Whatever procedure the builder followed, however, he went about his job with a sense of artistry and fine craftsmanship that is part of the built-in beauty of a classic boat.

For the builder of classic boats, these diagrams and tables are a guide to construction; for the classic-boat lover they are a blueprint to understanding such craft.

Creating the Basic Shape

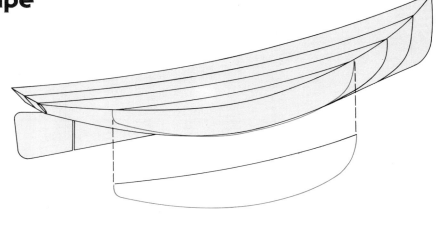

The direct relationship between a half model and a scale drawing for an actual Crosby catboat named *Frances*, built in 1900, is shown here and overleaf.

Imagine these half models sliced up evenly by a knife in different directions, so that one set of slices carved the hull into vertical, lengthwise strips; a second set cut through it from the side, parallel to the waterline; and the third set ran crosswise. With each cut, the knife would emerge from the hull along a contour line that followed the curve of the hull's surface. These three sets of contour lines describe the shape of the boat.

When drawing up the plans for a boat, a designer transcribes these lines—which are called buttocks, waterlines and sections respectively—onto three separate diagrams *(opposite)*, each showing the boat from a different perspective. The profile view depicts the boat from the side. The half-breadth view looks down from above. And the body plan is a split-image view, with one side showing the boat head-on from the bow, and the other giving a direct look from the stern. As a guide to the craft's final size, the designer inscribes the profile view over a base line, on which he marks down the exact overall length of the boat. He then measures off the base line into segments, called stations, upon which he positions the section lines. If the boat has a rounded bottom, he lays down still another set of lines called diagonals, which serve as a check on the accuracy of the other three sets of lines. As he makes each diagram, he correlates it with the previous diagrams and then combines them into a single drawing called a lines plan *(page 41)*.

One last element must be added to the lines plan before the boat's design is complete. This is a table of measurements, called offsets, which provides a precise, numerical description of the hull's shape. To get the offsets, the designer uses the body plan to measure off certain key hull distances. For example, the height of each buttock line above the base line, taken at the various stations along the hull, forms one such set of offsets. By using the measurements in the table of offsets, and with the diagrams in the lines plan as a visual guide, a builder can start the process of building a full-sized boat.

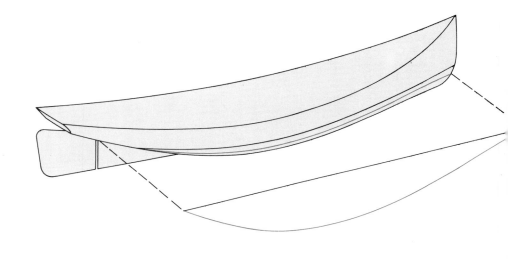

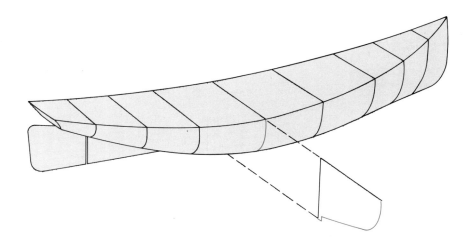

Profile

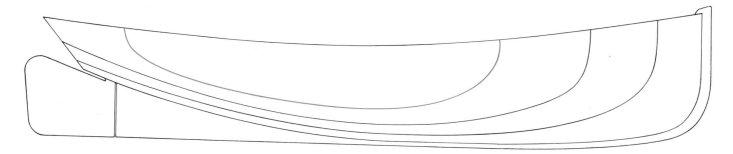

When the Crosby catboat's half model is cut into vertical lengthwise slices, the curved outside edge of each slice represents a contour line of the hull, as shown by the dark-blue edge of the vertical slice at left. Transcribed onto a profile view, this contour line becomes a buttock line (blue, above). Other, similarly conceived slices through the half model at carefully spaced intervals create a sequence of buttocks that precisely defines the boat's shape from this angle.

Half-Breadth

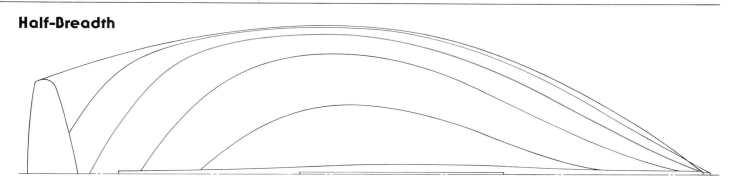

The waterlines, as their name suggests, run parallel to the boat's actual load waterline. The curved outer edge (blue, at left) of an imaginary horizontal slice through the half model represents one of the waterlines. Superimposed onto the half-breadth view of the Crosby cat, the waterline describes the boat's sharp entry at the bow, its extreme beaminess amidships and its gently curving stern.

Body Plan

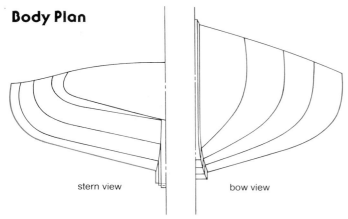

stern view   bow view

The outer edges of vertical slices made across the half model are the catboat's section lines. These are placed (above) on two images of the body plan—one a bow view, the other a stern view. Since the section in blue at left is aft of amidships, it appears only in the stern view; as on all lines plans, the outermost section in one of the two views—here the stern view—shows the hull's beamiest point.

Buttocks

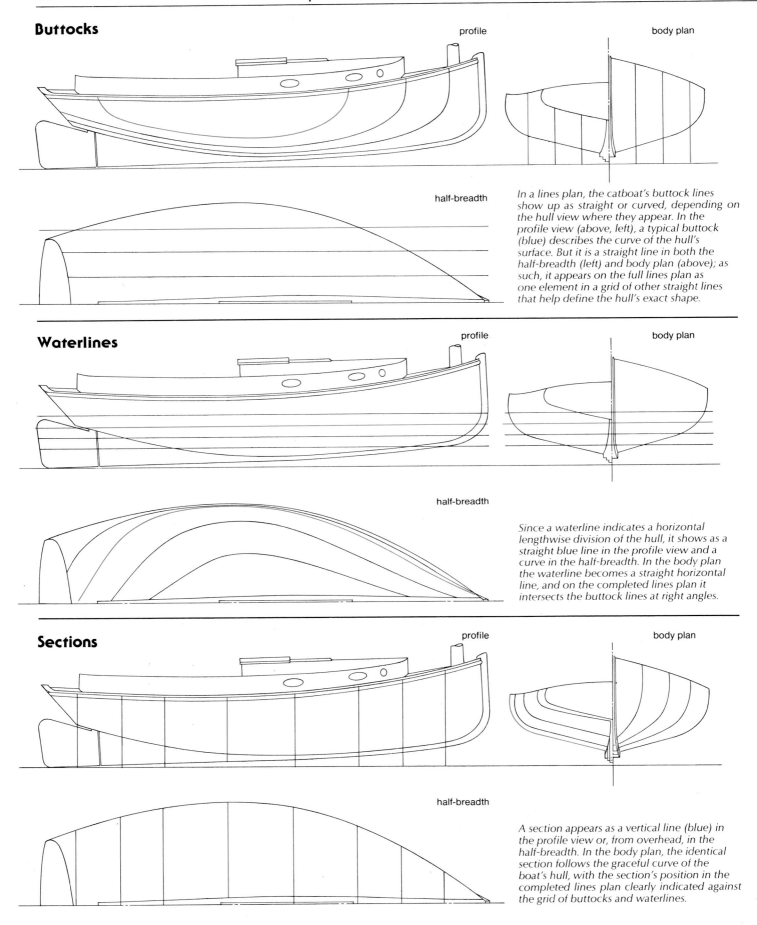

profile

body plan

half-breadth

In a lines plan, the catboat's buttock lines show up as straight or curved, depending on the hull view where they appear. In the profile view (above, left), a typical buttock (blue) describes the curve of the hull's surface. But it is a straight line in both the half-breadth (left) and body plan (above); as such, it appears on the full lines plan as one element in a grid of other straight lines that help define the hull's exact shape.

Waterlines

profile

body plan

half-breadth

Since a waterline indicates a horizontal lengthwise division of the hull, it shows as a straight blue line in the profile view and a curve in the half-breadth. In the body plan the waterline becomes a straight horizontal line, and on the completed lines plan it intersects the buttock lines at right angles.

Sections

profile

body plan

half-breadth

A section appears as a vertical line (blue) in the profile view or, from overhead, in the half-breadth. In the body plan, the identical section follows the graceful curve of the boat's hull, with the section's position in the completed lines plan clearly indicated against the grid of buttocks and waterlines.

Diagonals

The diagonals are added to the grid, as a check on the accuracy of the section lines. On the body plan a diagonal (blue) appears as a straight line; but from overhead it curves with the contour of the hull. The distances from the center line to the points of intersection between the diagonals and sections are the check points, which are listed numerically in the table of offsets on the lines plan below.

body plan

overhead

Catboat Frances
BUILT BY WILTON CROSBY, OSTERVILLE, MASS., 1900
LINES PLAN
LENGTH OVERALL : 20'8" BEAM : 9'8"

LINES TO OUTSIDE OF PLANKING

LINES TAKEN OFF AT MYSTIC SEAPORT, MAY 1966 BY E.J. SCHOCK
PLAN REDRAWN BY ROBERT A. PITTAWAY, AUGUST 1976
SCALE : 1" = 1'-0"

WATERLINES — SPACED 6" APART STARTING 12" ABOVE BASE LINE
BUTTOCKS — SPACED 15" APART STARTING AT CENTER LINE

DIAG. A — FROM 46" ABV ℄ ON ℄ TO 36" ABV ℄ ON BUTT. 45"
DIAG. B — FROM 42" ABV ℄ ON ℄ TO 18" ABV ℄ ON BUTT. 30"
DIAG. C — FROM 30" ABV ℄ ON ℄ TO 12" ABV ℄ ON BUTT. 15"

TABLE OF OFFSETS

	STATION	TRANS.	8	7	6	5	4	3	2	1	RABBET
HEIGHTS FROM BASE LINE (℄)	KEEL			0-1-2	0-2-0	0-3-3	0-4-5	0-6-3	0-8-3	0-11-2	
	RABBET	2-2-0	2-0-6	1-4-6	0-10-6	0-6-6	0-4-4	0-8-4	0-10-5	1-7-7	
	BUTT.15"	2-5-5	2-3-3	1-7-5	1-1-5	0-9-3	0-9-2	1-0-6	1-5-4	2-6-4	
	BUTT.30"	2-10-0	2-7-0	1-11-2	1-5-2	1-1-0	1-1-5	1-7-3	2-6-6		
	BUTT.45"		2-4-7	1-9-7	1-5-4	1-8-0					
	SHEER	3-7-6	3-6-0	3-4-2	3-3-3	3-5-6	3-10-1	4-2-3	4-7-3	5-0-0	
HALF BREADTHS FROM CENTER LINE (℄)	KEEL		0-0-6	0-1-6	0-2-3	0-3-4	0-3-6	0-2-6	0-2-3	0-2-0	
	RABBET	0-1-0	0-0-6	0-1-6	0-2-3	0-3-4	0-3-6	0-2-6	0-2-0	0-2-0	
	WL 12"			0-7-2	2-1-7	2-0-6	1-0-5	0-5-0			0-2-2
	WL 18"			0-7-1	2-9-1	3-10-0	2-3-1	1-3-7	0-5-4		0-1-6
	WL 24"		2-9-4	4-0-4	4-5-3	4-1-5	3-1-1	2-0-4	0-10-6		0-1-4
	WL 30"		1-5-6	3-10-2	4-4-3	4-7-7	4-4-3	3-5-6	2-5-6	0-10-0	0-1-0
	SHEER	2-11-0	3-4-7	3-11-6	4-4-6	4-8-0	4-5-3	3-7-4	2-8-2	1-6-2	0-1-0
DIAGONALS	DIAG.A	3-1-0	3-5-4	4-1-0	4-6-0	4-9-4	4-6-3	3-8-2			0-1-0
	DIAG.B	1-8-6	1-9-6	2-8-0	3-3-4	3-8-4	3-7-2	3-1-0	2-6-0	1-7-0	0-1-4
	DIAG.C	0-4-4	0-5-4	1-2-6	1-9-5	2-2-1	2-2-1	1-10-3	1-6-3	1-0-2	0-1-7

In the full lines plan of a Crosby catboat the profile view sits directly above a base line, marked by perpendiculars to indicate each section. Just below is the half-breadth, with waterlines and diagonals curving out from either side of the center line; the sections are marked off on the center line, as they are on the base line above. The body plan, with sections, diagonals, and grid of buttocks and waterlines, is at lower right. The table of offsets at lower left lists the key measurements from the center line or base line to the points where the sections cross the buttocks, waterlines and diagonals.

	STATION	TRANSOM	8	7	6	5	4	3	2	1	RABBET
HEIGHTS FROM BASE LINE (℔)	KEEL	—	—	0-1-2	0-2-0	0-3-3	0-4-5	0-6-3	0-8-3	0-11-2	—
	RABBET	2-2-0	2-0-6	1-4-6	0-10-6	0-6-6	0-6-4	0-8-4	0-10-5	1-1-2	—
	BUTT 15"	2-5-5	2-3-3	1-7-5	1-1-5	0-9-3	0-9-2	1-0-6	1-5-4	2-6-4	—
	BUTT 30"	2-10-0	2-7-0	1-11-2	1-5-2	1-1-0	1-1-5	1-7-3	2-6-6	—	—
	BUTT 45"	—	—	2-4-7	1-9-7	1-5-4	1-8-0	—	—	—	—
	SHEER	*3-7-6*	*3-6-0*	*3-4-2*	*3-3-2*	*3-3-3*	*3-5-6*	*3-10-1*	*4-2-3*	*4-7-3*	*5-0-0*
HALF BREADTHS FROM CENTER LINE (℄)	KEEL	—	0-0-6	0-1-6	0-2-3	0-3-4	0-3-6	0-2-6	0-2-3	0-2-0	—
	RABBET	0-1-0	0-0-6	0-1-6	0-2-3	0-3-4	0-3-6	0-2-6	0-2-3	0-2-0	—
	WL 12"	—	—	—	0-7-2	2-1-7	2-0-6	1-0-6	0-5-0	—	0-2-2
	WL 18"	—	—	0-7-1	2-9-1	3-10-0	3-5-4	2-3-1	1-3-7	0-5-4	0-1-6
	WL 24"	—	—	2-9-1	4-0-4	4-5-3	4-1-5	3-1-1	2-0-4	0-10-6	0-1-4
	WL 30"	1-5-6	2-1-6	3-10-2	4-4-3	4-7-7	4-4-5	3-5-4	2-5-5	1-2-7	0-1-1
	SHEER	2-11-0	3-4-7	3-11-6	4-4-6	4-8-0	4-5-3	3-7-4	2-8-2	1-5-2	0-1-0
DIAGONALS	DIAG A	3-1-0	3-5-4	4-1-0	4-6-0	4-9-4	4-6-3	3-8-2	2-9-0	1-6-2	0-1-0
	DIAG B	1-8-6	1-9-6	2-8-0	3-3-4	3-8-4	3-7-2	3-1-0	2-6-0	1-7-0	0-1-4
	DIAG C	0-4-4	0-5-4	1-2-6	1-9-5	2-2-1	2-2-1	1-10-3	1-6-3	1-0-2	0-1-7

Each notation on the table of offsets above serves as a reference point for drafting one of the lines on the lofting. To determine the sheer line on the profile view, for example, the builder looks along the first row of entries titled "sheer" (blue). The numbers in each entry give the distance in feet, inches and eighth inches between the sheer line and the base line at the designated station. At station 7, for instance, this distance will be 3 feet 4¼ inches. The builder marks off this point (X on the loft plan below) and every other point in the row of entries. By connecting these points, he is able to draw in the sheer line.

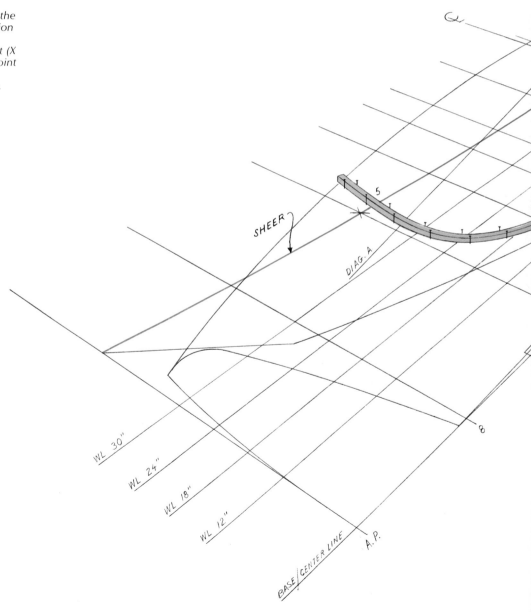

The lofting for the Cape Cod catboat contains the profile, half-breadth and body plan, superimposed one atop the other on the loft floor to save space. The vertical section lines and horizontal waterlines of the profile view create the grid on which the boat's profile shape is drafted. The sheer line derived from the offsets (left) appears in blue. The builder has begun the half-breadth and he has started drawing the body plan. A flexible batten for fairing Section 5 of the body plan runs along a set of points taken from the middle group of figures in the Section 5 column of the offsets; the batten is held in place by a pair of nails driven into the loft floor at each point.

Scaling Up to Size

When a boatwright starts to create an actual boat, his first step is to scale the lines plan up to full size so that he can create patterns for shaping the hull. Often working directly on a loft floor, he marks off the boat's base line. With the base line as his index he then draws—in outline—the full-size profile view: first the gridwork of vertical section lines and horizontal waterlines, and then the curved sheer and keel lines. The straight lines are fairly simple to render, but the curved lines require some expertise. The builder must consult the table of offsets *(far left)* and use the entries to measure off a series of points on the loft floor. He next takes a flexible wooden batten and connects the points. If a point lies slightly to one side of the batten—indicating an error in the offsets—the builder must fair the line. That is, he moves the point to meet the batten, and remembers to make the same correction when drawing the subsequent views.

Next, the builder outlines the half-breadth and he drafts the entire body plan. Then he completes the two outlined views, fairing each line and making sure it agrees with the same line on the body plan. Finally, using the profile view and body plan, he can start cutting the lumber to build his boat, which often includes a set of wooden molds like the one below.

To shape the catboat's hull during construction, the boatwright builds wooden molds, like the one shown here, that he will fit onto the keel at each hull section. To make a mold, the builder finds the corresponding curved section line on the lofted body plan, and transfers it to scrap lumber. Generally the line describes the outside of the hull, so he deducts the thickness of the planking before he marks the wood. Then he cuts out the pieces, nails or cleats them together, and braces them with a cross-spall. He notches the mold to grip the keel, and marks the center, load water- and sheer lines to orient the mold on the keel and to help position the top planks.

The Basic Carpentry

After a boatbuilder has established his craft's basic hull shape through his lofting of the lines plan, he turns to the final set of drawings—the construction plan. This plan supplies what are known as the boat's scantlings—the dimensions of individual planks and timbers—as well as the kind of lumber required for each, and the key carpentry details he will need to know when fitting the pieces together.

Using the construction plan and the lofted lines plan as guides, the building of most boats follows a fairly standard sequence. First the builder assembles the backbone (right)—including the centerboard trunk, if the boat has one. For any boat in which the frames must be bent to the curve of the hull, as on the catboat here, he sets up a temporary framework (opposite). The basis of the framework is the series of wooden molds fashioned from the sections in the loft plan. To these are fastened horizontal wooden strips called ribbands. Inside the ribbands, the builder lays the frames and fits them into the keel as specified by the construction plan. Then he starts putting on the planks, removing the ribbands as he goes. Finally, he knocks out the molds, and the basic hull is complete.

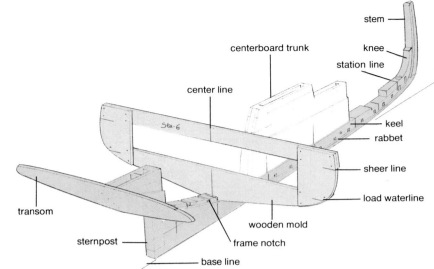

The backbone of a boat consists of the stem, keel and stern members; during construction, it is carefully positioned over a base line below it. To assemble this catboat, the builder first cuts a groove, or rabbet, into the keel and stem pieces to receive the planking; he then notches the keel for the frames, and attaches the stem. He bolts on the transom and centerboard trunk. Next he fits the molds onto the keel, centering each on a station line taken from the loft plan.

On the catboat construction plan shown here, the major structural members are tinted blue for easy identification—as they are in the drawings above and on the opposite page. The sizes and shapes of the backbone timbers are detailed on the profile view, which shows the completed hull split lengthwise, with its major elements in place and their scantlings written nearby. Scantlings for frames and planking are given in the cross-section views above the profile view.

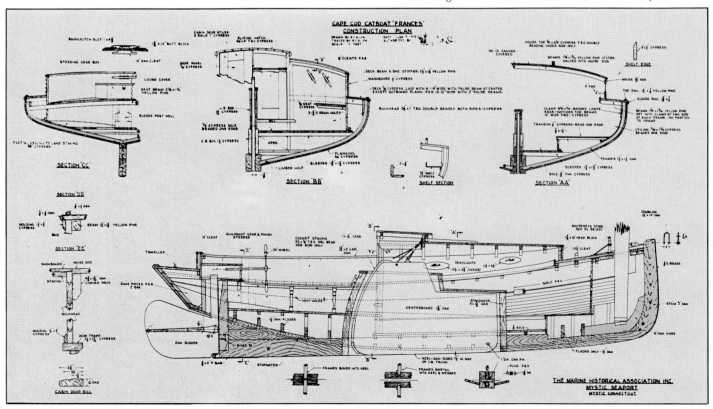

Once the molds are all fixed to the backbone, the next major step in construction is to temporarily attach ribbands to every mold from stem to transom. The ribbands help support the molds, but their primary function is to provide a stationary form against which the builder can bend the frames to shape—after they have been softened in a steam box (page 51). In this illustration, the builder has already fastened on the three aftermost frames, each cut from 1½-by-1½-inch oak, as indicated in Section "AA" of the construction plan.

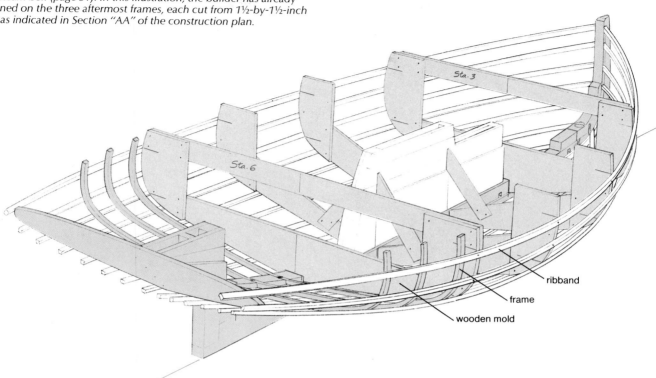

ribband

frame

wooden mold

With the frames in place, the builder reinforces the juncture between the frames and keel with timbers called floors. Then comes the last stage in fashioning the basic hull: attaching the planking. This is done with the molds in place—though here they have been omitted for clarity. The builder first removes the two ribbands nearest the keel, and in their place attaches the two garboard strakes. He puts on the two adjoining planks, and then jumps to the two sheer strakes. The subsequent planks go on in the same manner—lower strakes, then upper strakes, first a plank on one side, then one on the other, until the final plank, called the shutter, is slid into place.

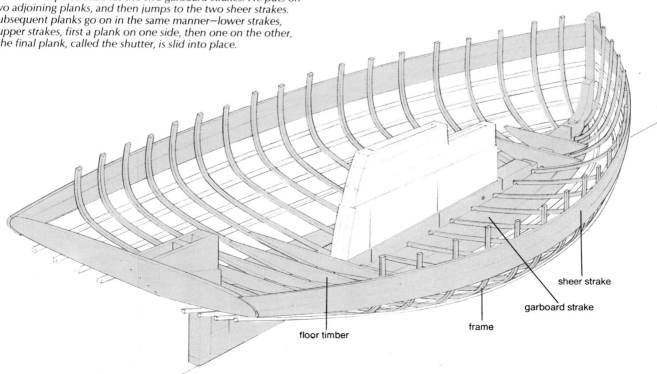

sheer strake

garboard strake

floor timber

frame

A cutaway view of the Cape Cod catboat shows the complex
interlocking of parts that make up its hull. The frames are wedged
into notches in the keel; the frames' upper ends are held between the
clamp, the covering board and the sheer strake. The deck beams,
which support the decking, run between the clamp and a thin piece
of trim called a facia piece. Some of the floors are notched to fit
atop the keel. The rudder construction is typical of larger boats with
overhanging transoms: the rudder post runs between a pair of
rake pieces into a steering box, to connect with a tiller or wheel.

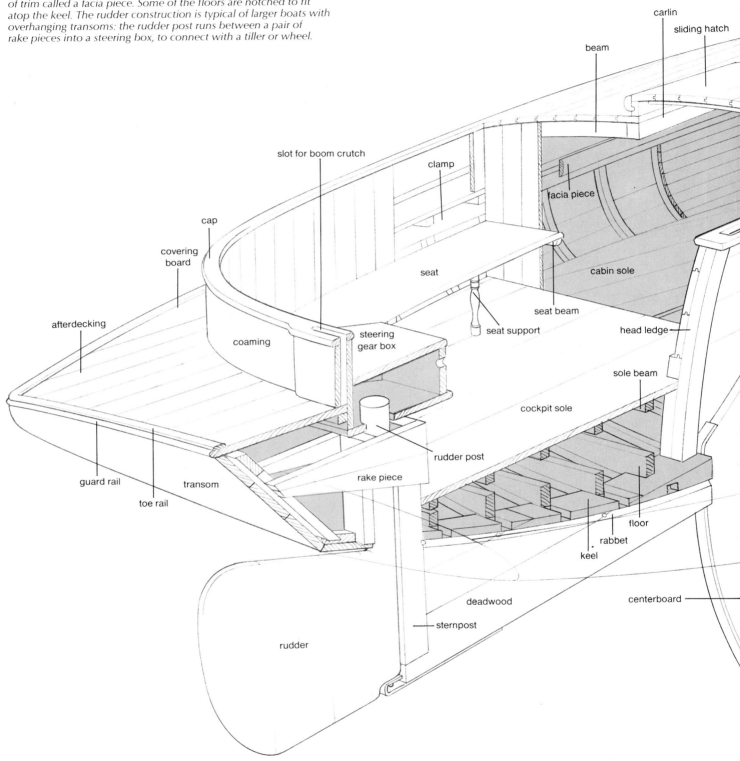

The Final Assembly

Once the builder has assembled a boat's structural members, he joins to them a multitude of other parts to complete the hull. In a medium-sized craft like this 21-foot Crosby catboat these pieces may number in the hundreds. Nearly every one does double or triple duty. A covering board, for instance, is both the working surface of the deck and a protection for the sawed-off upper ends of the frames. These frame ends are held securely in place by a long, heavy timber called the clamp, which also supports the outboard ends of the deck beams.

The functions of a few pieces of a boat's anatomy are clear from their names. A cap serves to shelter something from the weather; here the centerboard trunk and cockpit coaming are both capped. But the names of other parts are anything but revealing: a rabbet is a lengthwise groove cut into one piece of wood so that another piece can be fitted to it. A rabbet in the keel accepts the lowermost plank, or garboard. A boat's floors are strengthening timbers along the keel. The ceiling is the planking that covers the inside of the cabin. Limber holes are notches that let water run freely along the bilges. A carlin supports the inboard ends of deck beams where there is an opening in the deck.

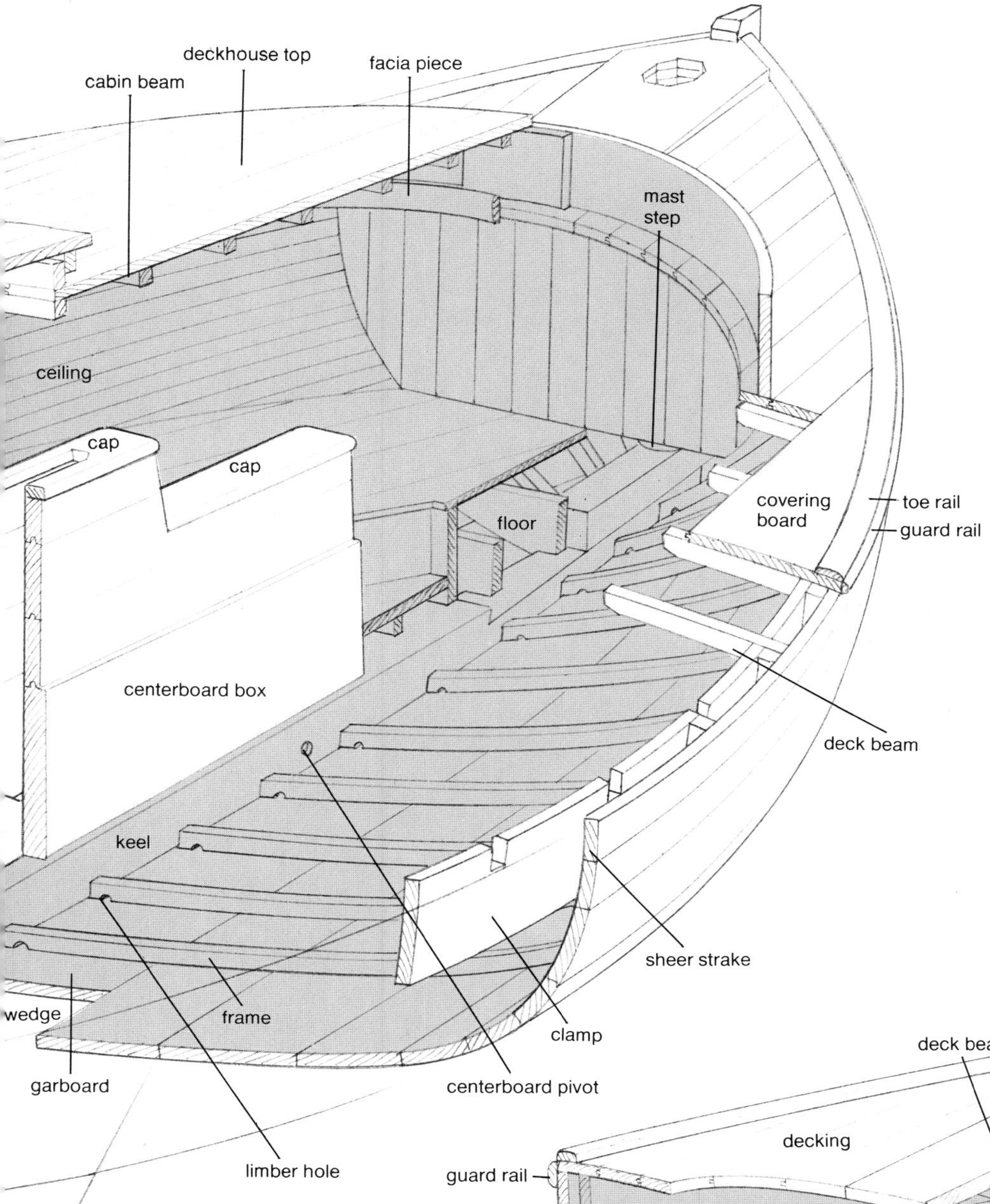
deckhouse top
cabin beam
facia piece
mast step
ceiling
cap
cap
floor
covering board
toe rail
guard rail
centerboard box
deck beam
keel
sheer strake
wedge
frame
clamp
garboard
centerboard pivot
limber hole

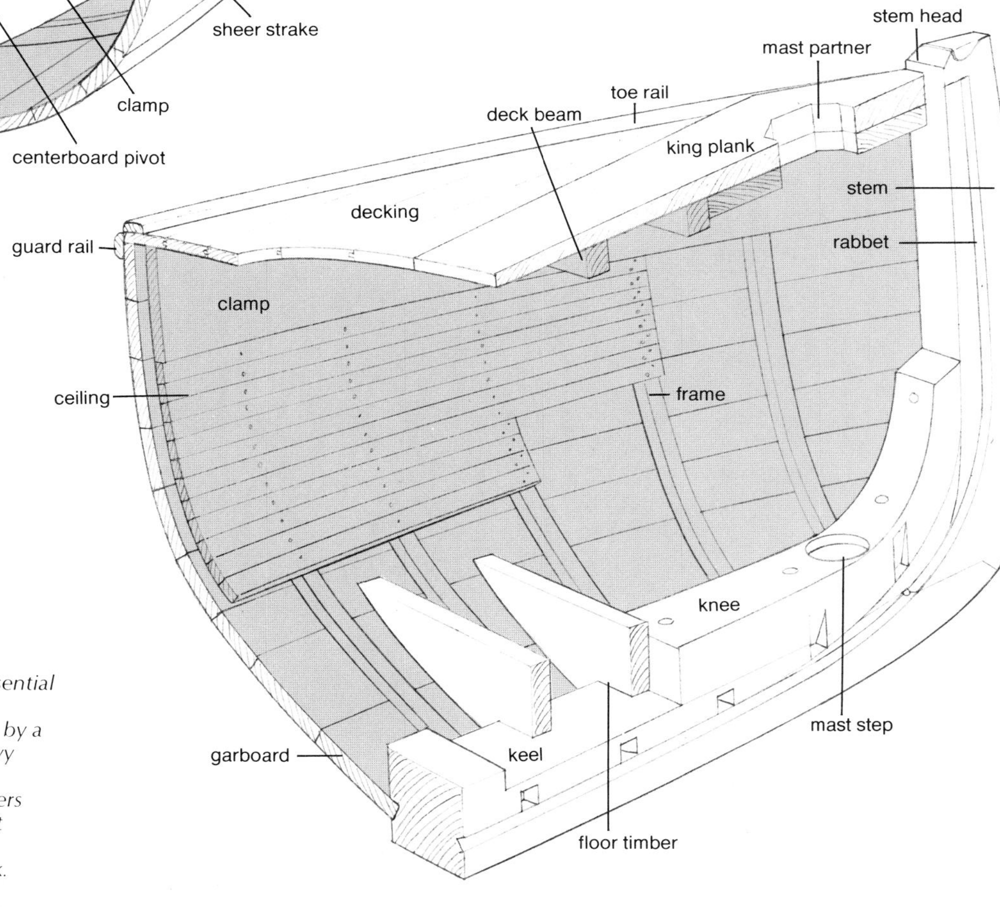
stem head
mast partner
toe rail
deck beam
king plank
stem
decking
rabbet
guard rail
clamp
ceiling
frame
knee
mast step
garboard
keel
floor timber

This extra-sturdy bow construction is essential on catboats, in order to secure the mast, which is otherwise held in position only by a single stay. The mast is stepped in a heavy curved knee, which also forms a brace between the stem and keel. Heavy timbers called the partners buttress the mast as it emerges through the deck by way of a heavy central piece called the king plank.

Variations on the Backbone

Though the creation of nearly every boat in classic times followed the same general guidelines, the shapes, makeup and constructional details might vary enormously from one vessel to another. This was particularly true of a vessel's single most important structural member: the backbone, whose keel, stern and stem components might be cut and fastened together in scores of different configurations. For example, a Friendship sloop's backbone *(right)* typically was made up of twice as many pieces as that of the Cape Cod catboat on page 44. And these boats were only two of the hundreds of distinct classic boat types and subtypes whose shapes changed not only from region to region, but from builder to builder.

The after portion of the backbone *(bottom, left)* might have been a simple transom abutting the bottom planking, as in the rudderless Noank skiff from eastern Connecticut, or a more complex arrangement as in the more modern, motorized fishing launch, whose large rudder and propeller required special support pieces.

The keel *(bottom, center),* as well as supplying the hull's main longitudinal strength, usually provided a bearing surface to which the garboard planks fastened. The groove, or rabbet, often cut to accommodate the garboard planking, ran the length of the keel and into the bow and stern sections. At the bow, the boat's stem *(bottom, right)* took up where the keel left off, and was attached to it in one of several ways, each designed to maintain strength in this inherently weak, often curving, portion of the backbone.

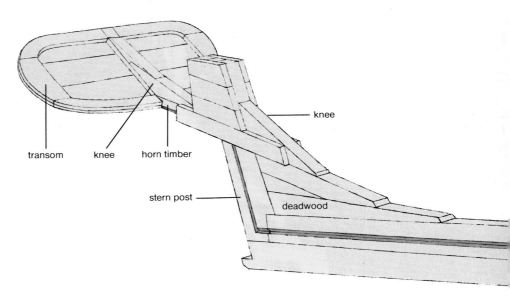

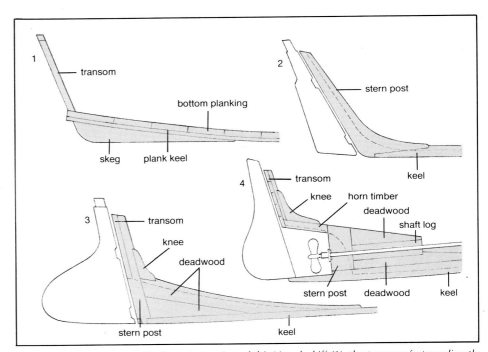

In the stern section of this Noank skiff (1), the transom fastens directly to the bottom planking, and a small skeg is fastened to an exterior plank keel. The double-ended No Mans Land boat (2) has no transom; a rabbet (dotted line) was cut into the stern post to receive the side planks. The hefty stern of a Connecticut River drag boat (3) carries a small deadwood area, ending in a vertical stern post that supports the transom and a knee. Even sturdier is this motorized fishing launch (4). The deadwood, cut back to make room for a propeller, provides a shaft log and is strengthened by a thick stern post. A horn timber, held to the transom by a knee, supports the boat's counter.

Massive timbers of hewn oak are fitted together to form the complex backbone of a Friendship sloop. The keel consists of two pieces—an outer keel and a heavy inner keel bolted to it for additional strength. At the bow, the joint between this composite keel and the stem is buttressed along its outboard edge by a stout filler piece, and inboard by an enormous knee, which also serves as a mast step. Above the filler is an outer stem piece and timber called the billethead that forms the clipper bow. In the stern, three adjoining timbers form the deadwood—the large skeglike area designed to help the sloop track through the water when it is under sail. A hefty vertical stern post attaches to the deadwood and to the keel. A horizontal piece called a horn timber supports the overhanging stern or counter. A stern knee reinforces the connection between the horn timber and the raked transom; another is set between the rudder post and deadwood.

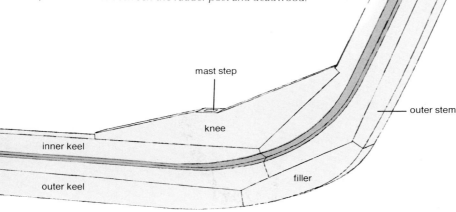

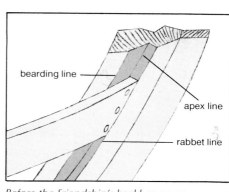

Before the Friendship's backbone was assembled, a rabbet was cut into the keel, stem and stern sections to accept the planking. In this detail, the plank butts against the face between the groove's outer edge, or rabbet line, and its apex line. The plank fastens between the apex and bearding lines. The rabbet's shape varies from place to place along the backbone, depending on the angle at which the plank meets it.

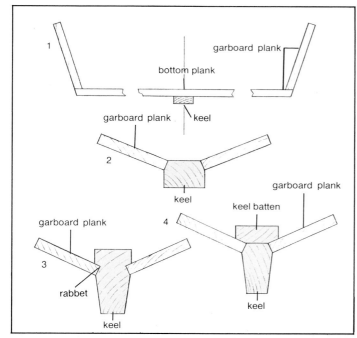

Many small flat-bottomed boats (1) were built with exterior plank-type keels to reinforce their cross-planked bottoms. In other hull shapes, the keel acted as a longitudinal support, as well as an anchor for the garboard planks. In round-bottomed boats with slack-bilged or flat sections (2), the garboard planks butted up against beveled edges cut along the top of the keel. But deeper, shapelier hulls required a rabbet, usually chiseled into the solid keel (3), to give the planks greater fastening surface. As an alternative to this difficult cut, the builder could bevel the edges of two separate pieces—a keel batten and the keel—and put them together to create the proper groove (4).

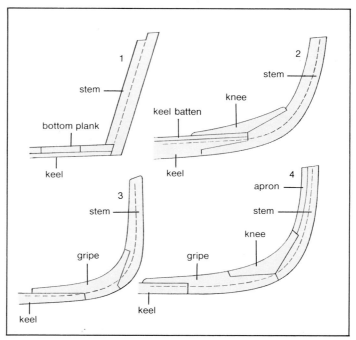

The stem in this sharpie-type skiff (1) meets the keel at nearly right angles and attaches to it directly with no special supports. A peapod's curved stem (2) overlaps the keel and keel batten, and the joint requires a small knee for added strength. To help create the much sharper curve in the stem of a Connecticut River drag boat (3), an intermediate member called a gripe connects the keel and stem; the gripe's long arms assure that the stem and keel are securely attached. In a Whitehall (4), both a stem knee and a Z-shaped gripe add strength to the stem-keel connection. A piece behind the stem called an apron provides additional surface for fastening the planks.

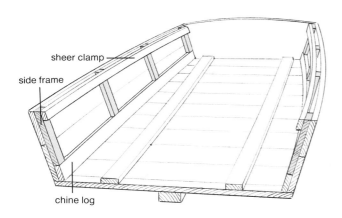

sheer clamp

side frame

chine log

This section of a New Jersey garvey—an elementary scow-type hull used for shoal-water fishing and freighting—shows the simple side frames used in most flat-bottomed boats. The cross-planking of the garvey's bottom eliminated the need for bottom frames—and made the boats easy and cheap to build. These frames started at the chine log and ran up the sides to the sheer, where they were held in place by a sheer clamp. For added rigidity the frames of some flat-bottomed craft notched over the chine log and sheer clamp.

The frames of a Long Island skipjack—a V-bottomed adaptation of local inshore fishing sloops—were fashioned from two separate pieces of wood. The short side frames began at the sheer—their tops held in place by a sheer clamp—and turned inboard at the chine, where they were side-fastened to bottom frames. The bottom frames, which held together the fore-and-aft bottom planks, then continued on to the keel where they fastened to a floor timber. On most other V-bottomed boats, where the bottom planks were run athwartships to save time and production costs, no bottom frames were necessary.

sheer clamp

chine

side frame

bottom frame

floor timber

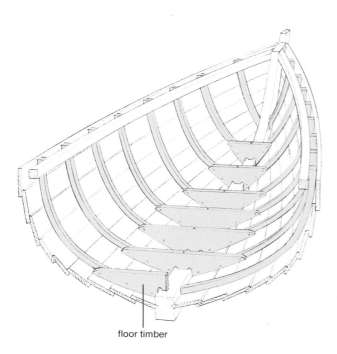

floor timber

On the round-bottomed No Mans Land boat at left—designed to sail in the stiff winds and confused seas off Martha's Vineyard—the frames were generally steamed to make them pliable and then bent to conform to the shape of the hull, as in the example here. This was the quickest method, although some builders in the Vineyard Sound area where this model originated sawed the frames to shape to provide a somewhat stronger construction. In either case, the builder firmly anchored the frames at the keel with floor timbers.

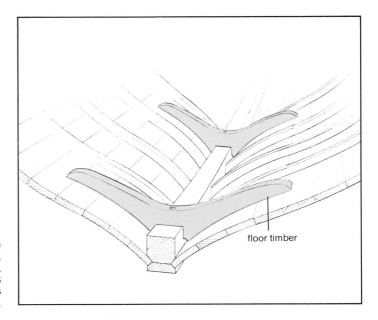

floor timber

The floor timbers of this Tancook whaler from Nova Scotia show a common variation in the structural bonding between a boat's frames, planking and keel. Rather than fastening directly to the frames, the floors served to strengthen the lower few hull planks between frames. The hull planks, held securely in place by the floor's long arms, kept the frame heels firmly anchored at the keel.

Framing the Hull

A boat's frames run at right angles to its backbone and make up the next most important element in its skeleton. They add stiffness to the hull, and help to hold the planking in place. And like the backbone, they differ enormously in their size, shape and basic structure from one variety of craft to another—and from boatyard to boatyard. A surfboat builder on the New Jersey coast, for example, customarily endowed his beachable craft with far heftier frames than did the builder of an Adirondack guide boat designed for rowing on inland mountain lakes.

The type of frames the builder chose depended primarily on the shape of the hull. Most flat-bottomed boats, such as the scowlike garvey *(far left, top)*, required no bottom frames and needed only vertical stiffening pieces along the sides of the hull. These simple side frames were also sufficient for most V-bottomed boats—although some, like the Long Island skipjack *(near left, top)*, had separate bottom frames that ran from the keel to the side frames. And any round-bottomed vessel such as the No Mans Land boat *(far left, bottom)* generally had a series of curved, riblike frames that began at the keel and ran up the sides to the sheers.

Wherever the frames extended all the way to the keel, the builder often fastened their bottoms, or heels, to a crosspiece called a floor timber, which was in turn fastened to the keel. The floor timbers anchored the frame heels in place and added strength to the lower few rows of planking *(near left, bottom)*.

To make frames, the builder either sawed them to shape or steamed them in a steam box and bent them to shape.

In one method of making frames—especially for round-bottomed boats—the builder sawed them out of natural crooks of wood (below, left), such as a large tree root. The cut would follow the curved grain of the wood, thus giving the frame strength and durability. When the builder had no single crook large enough for fashioning the entire frame, he cut two or more separate pieces—called futtocks— which he then joined together with a wood cleat (below, right).

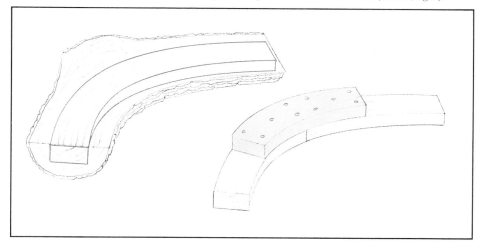

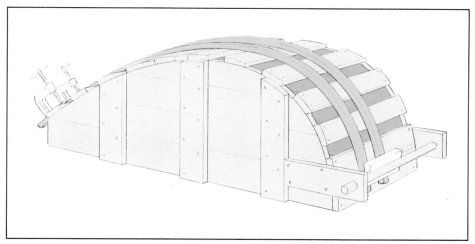

A Carpenter's Steam Box

A steam box like the one at left permitted the builder to soften straight pieces of hardwood temporarily so that they could be bent or twisted to suit the curves in a boat's hull. A typical box like this one could be knocked together easily. A large kettle on a wood-burning stove supplied the steam and was connected to the box by a hose or pipe. To keep steam in the box, its seams were packed with rags or cotton caulking.

To get frames ready for steaming, the builder soaked the stock—green, winter-cut oak was best—in water for two or three days. He then placed the frames in the box and left them there about one hour for every inch of a frame's thickness. The builder commonly would steam a half-dozen or so frames at one time.

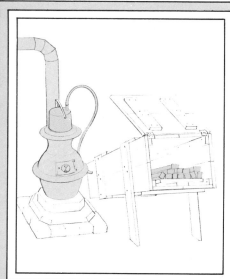

In the most common method of making frames for round-bottomed boats, boatbuilders steamed hardwoods such as white oak in a steam box (left) and then bent the wood to shape. With the aid of two or three men, the builder could take the frames directly from the steam box and bend them into the hull while they were still hot and pliable. Working alone, the builder first had to shape the hot frames over a mold, called a trap (above), built to represent an exaggeration of the sharpest curve in the hull. Then, he clamped the cooled frames into the hull, forcing out any excess curve by hand.

Planking and Fastenings

The nature of a boat's hull planking, like every other important structural component, depended on the shape and function of the hull, the lumber stock available, the predominant boatbuilding traditions in the region—and, ultimately, the whims of the boatwright. Among the score or so methods of planking a hull, the two most used were carvel and lapstrake. Carvel, or smooth, planking, shown at left, top, provided hulls with thick, tough skins that were relatively easy to repair—an important economic consideration to a self-employed fisherman. Lapstraking (left, below) tended to be used in smaller boats when a combination of strength and lightness was called for.

Some of the other planking methods (below) were more complex, but they offered some improvements over carvel and lapstrake. Strip building added strength to hulls with difficult curves in their shapes; double planking was very long lasting and perhaps the strongest of all ways of planking; batten seam construction minimized leakage in hulls that were kept out of the water for long periods of time.

Although in most small-boat construction a single plank would cover the distance from stem to stern, in larger boats, builders often had to use more than one plank to complete a strake. In this case, a so-called butt block (right, middle) reinforced the joint where the two planks met. (An alternative to butt blocks, called plank scarphing, is described on page 59.) To fasten planks in place against frames and backbone, builders used an assortment of galvanized-iron or copper fastenings, ranging from the hefty boat nail to the copper rivet (right, top).

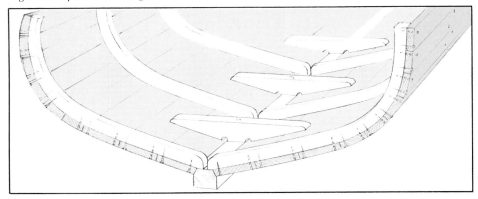

Carvel planks like those shown here from a section of an Albemarle Sound shad-seining boat, lie against one another edge to edge to form a smooth outer hull surface. The strakes are attached at each of the frames, with the fastenings set close to the seams to keep the edges of the planks close together and help make the hull watertight.

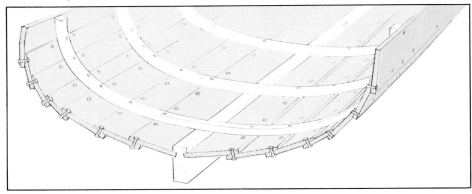

Planks on a lapstrake, or clinker-built, boat, like the Providence River boat below, were lapped over one another instead of being laid edge to edge, as in carvel planking. The boatbuilder fastened the strakes together where they overlapped, adding great longitudinal strength to the hull—which, as a result, needed fewer and lighter frames. This strong but lightweight construction was excellent for any boat that frequently had to be hauled up on davits or beached.

In strip building, the edge-fastening of each strake to its neighbor created a strong unified hull, and nearly eliminated the need for frames. With super-strong double planking, the builder had to measure, cut and fit two separate but staggered layers of carvel planks. In a hull that had batten seam planking, wooden battens backed up the plank seams and reduced the amount of potential shrinkage when the hull was out of the water. The seam battens also served as longitudinal reinforcement for the hull.

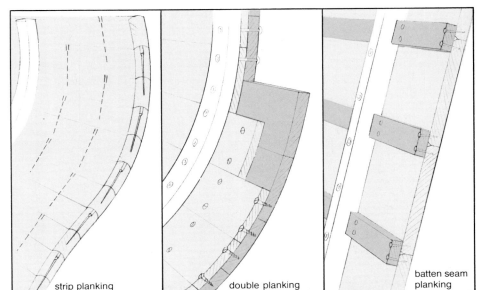

strip planking   double planking   batten seam planking

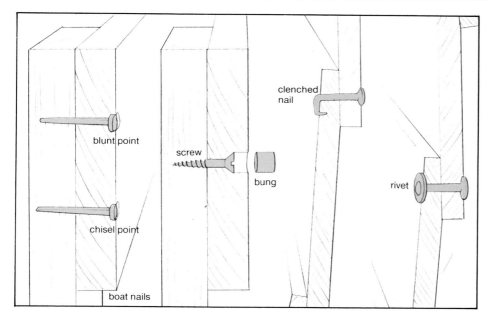

boat nails

To hold hulls together, boatbuilders used a range of specialized fastenings. Perhaps the commonest was the rectangular-shanked, blunt- or chisel-pointed, galvanized-iron boat nail. A boat nail had great holding power, except in softwoods or in thinner materials where screws—countersunk and bunged —were used. In lapstraking, planks were fastened with so-called clenched nails, whose points were bent back into the wood on the inside of the boat. The copper rivet, another lapstrake fastening, was made by nipping short the end of a copper nail and splaying it over a copper washer called a rove.

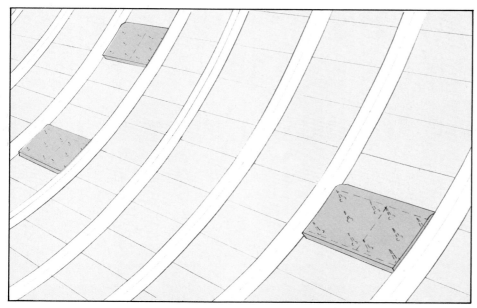

Butt blocks, joining the ends of two planks, traditionally measured 12 times the planking thickness in length to give the joint strength. The butt blocks overlapped the planks' width by ½ inch on either side to keep the butted planks from pulling the butt block out, and were cut off short of the frames at both ends to create a channel for water drainage. For overall hull strength, the butts in adjacent strakes were set three frame spaces apart, and those in the same frame space were separated by three to four strakes.

Log-Canoe Joinery

Chesapeake Bay log canoes, built according to regional tradition dating back to colonial times, had no true planks. Instead, builders adapted the single-log Indian dugout design and shaped their own canoe hulls from three or more pine logs. After adzing the logs to shape, and planing their joints smooth, the builders edge-fastened them in one of the several ways shown at right. The oldest type of fastening, called treenails, consisted of wooden dowels that were wedged into holes bored at mating locations in adjacent logs. In place of treenails, some early builders used iron dowels. In a third method the builder placed butterfly-shaped oak plates across the seams —both inboard and outboard—and held them in place with wooden pins.

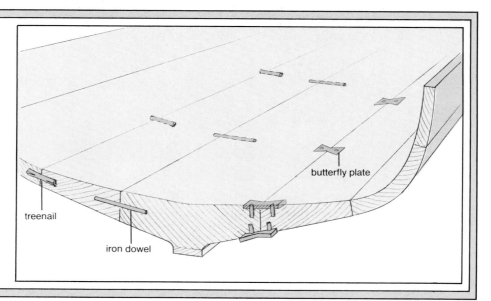

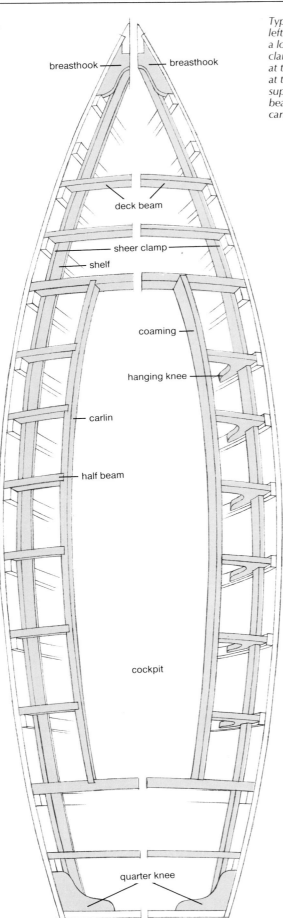

Typical deck-framing systems appear in the split-apart diagrams at left. In the diagram of the starboard side, the builder has used a longitudinal timber called a sheer clamp; the port side has a sheer clamp plus another fore-and-aft member called a shelf. Both are held at the stem by a horizontal, V-shaped knee called a breasthook, and at the transom by so-called quarter knees. Athwartships deck beams support full decks in both systems; half-deck supports are either half-beams (port) or knees (starboard). Fore-and-aft pieces such as carlins (port) and coamings (starboard) support the deck openings.

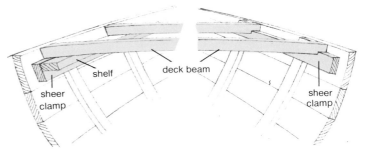

To support planking in a fully decked area, such as the foredeck, the builder cut deck beams the full width of the hull. He could fasten them either to a sheer clamp (above, right) or to a sheer clamp and shelf (above, left). As additional support, the builder often side-fastened the beams to the tops of frames.

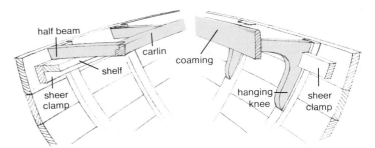

For any deck opening such as a cockpit, the builder could support the half decks by either of the two methods shown here. In some boats a fore-and-aft member called a carlin (above, left) held up the inboard side of the half deck, and half beams, notched into the carlins, supported the deck planks. Other construction methods called for a deep coaming (above, right) to replace the carlin, and hanging knees to replace the half beams.

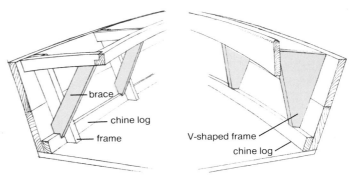

To support the half decks in flat- and V-bottomed boats, some boatbuilders used one of these two methods. In the first, wooden struts angle out from the base of the frame at the chine log to brace the inboard edge of the deck. In the other method, the builder tapered the frame itself so that its top edge was wide enough to take the deck planks.

Building the Deck

As the final step in the basic construction of all but small open boats, the builder tied the hull together at deck level with a framework of longitudinal and athwartship timbers *(far left)*. This framework not only kept the boat's topsides from sagging outward, but also served to support the vessel's deck planks.

To stiffen the hull at the sheer, the builder added fore-and-aft members such as sheer clamps and shelves, which were secured at the stem and stern with horizontally placed knees. Over these longitudinal pieces the builder laid the deck beams *(near left, at top)*, running them from sheer to sheer and usually cutting them to a slight arc for a cambered deck. When an open area such as a cockpit interrupted the deck, half beams, hanging knees or special frames replaced the full beams to support the half decks *(near left, center and bottom)*. Structural members such as carlins or coamings gave the opening longitudinal strength.

Over the finished framing system, the builder fit and fastened the deck planks *(right)* and made them watertight *(below, left)*. To complete the decking, the builder fastened on finishing pieces such as toe rails and sheer guards *(below, right)*.

Once the deck framing was completed, the builder fit the deck planks to the shape of the hull in one of two ways. In straight decking *(below, left)*, with planking laid parallel to the boat's center line, he began at the deck's center and worked out to the sides where the planks were shaped to meet the covering boards—wide planks cut to fit the sheer—with either so-called shim (1) or nibbed (2) ends. For sprung decking *(below, right)*, the builder bent, or sprung, the planks to fit the hull shape, beginning at the covering boards and ending at the central, or king, plank with either shim (3) or nibbed (4) ends.

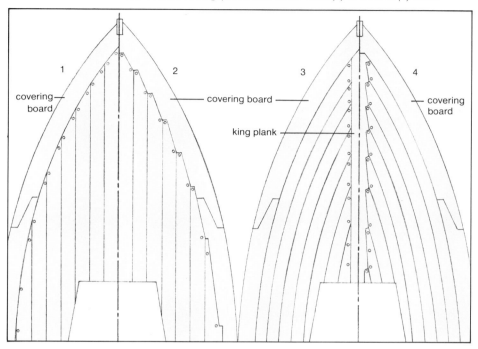

The cheapest and most quickly fit planking—used only for straight decks—was tongue-and-groove stock *(top)*. To make a tongue-and-groove deck watertight, canvas was stretched over a heavy coat of white lead paint on the deck, tacked down and then painted; often the canvas had to be seamed together—using the overlapping method shown above—to make up the deck's width. Plain, laid planks *(above, at bottom)* were used for either straight or sprung decking, depending on their dimensions—nearly square in section for sprung decking. For watertightness, laid decks were caulked as shown here.

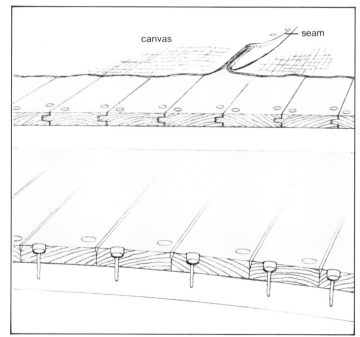

As the last important step in decking a boat, the builder finished off the exterior of the hull at deck level. On the side planking at the sheer he fastened a half-round strip called a sheer guard. The sheer guard not only protected the hull from bumps and scrapes, but also covered up the seam between the deck planking and the sheer strake, and secured the end of the canvas in a canvas-covered deck. At the edge of the decking, or slightly inboard of it, the builder fastened a finishing piece called a toe rail. To allow spray and rain water to drain overboard, scuppers were cut into the toe rails.

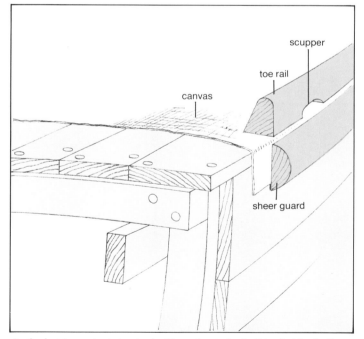

Fisherman's Friend: The Dory

Most American workboats, like the Grand Banks dory shown here and the craft on the following eight pages, were built for specialized purposes. To serve those ends, they were put together in marvelously inventive ways that always gave a distinctive personality to each craft type.

The Grand Banks dory, for example, was developed in the mid-1800s for fishing the banks some 100 miles off the coast of Newfoundland. At the fishing grounds, the fishermen would lower the dories into the North Atlantic, where one- or two-man crews hand-lined for cod or halibut.

Built of stout 9/16-inch white pine planking, and 1-by-2-inch oak timbers, a typical 18-footer like the one shown here could be knocked together by a professional builder in just eight to 12 hours. The dory has only four planks on each side, lapstraked for strength—and to make it watertight without caulking. Its bottom is made up of only three planks, secured by wooden cleats running athwartships. The frames, too, are simplicity itself. Each one consists of two nearly straight pieces of oak, joined by a galvanized-iron clip—with no complex sawing or bending required. Finally, an ingenious false stem *(opposite, center)* eliminates the need for complex joinery work at the bow.

The completed dory is perfectly adapted for being carried aboard a mother ship and then put into open water for prolonged fishing. With flared topsides and removable thwarts, a half-dozen dories could be nested one inside the other on the deck of a schooner, forming a stack about six feet high and no wider than the beam of a single boat. Once in the water, the craft's high, peaked ends and topsides flare kept it relatively dry in rough seas —even with a full 1,500-pound load of fish aboard. So practical was the design and construction of this dory that, like the craft on pages 58-65, it can still be found plying America's boating waters.

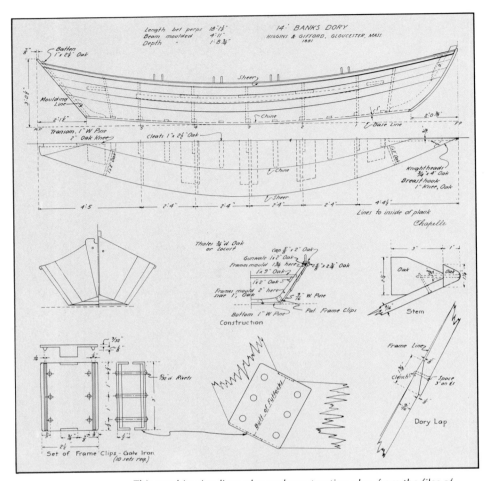

This combination lines plan and construction plan, from the files of the Smithsonian Institution in Washington, D.C., contains virtually all the information an experienced builder needs to duplicate a Grand Banks dory. The hull views give not only the boat's lines, but also the locations of the frames and athwartship cleats. Construction details include specifications for frames and thwarts in the cross section at center; the false stem in the diagram to its right; galvanized-iron frame clips at lower left and center; and in the lower right corner, the dory's specialized type of lapstraking, called dory lap.

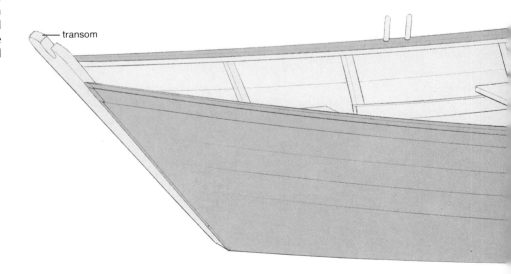

transom

To give the dory its characteristic rockered bottom, the builder used braces to force the bottom planks into shape. With the planks secured by cleats, and the transom and stem in place, the builder nailed a wooden strut like the one here to each mold. He then wedged the strut's upper end against a ceiling beam to exert downward pressure (large arrow). Upward pressure (small arrows) came from wooden blocks driven under the bow and stern, which raised them above the floor to a height indicated in the lines plan. Then, as the builder put on the planking, the rocker was literally nailed into the hull.

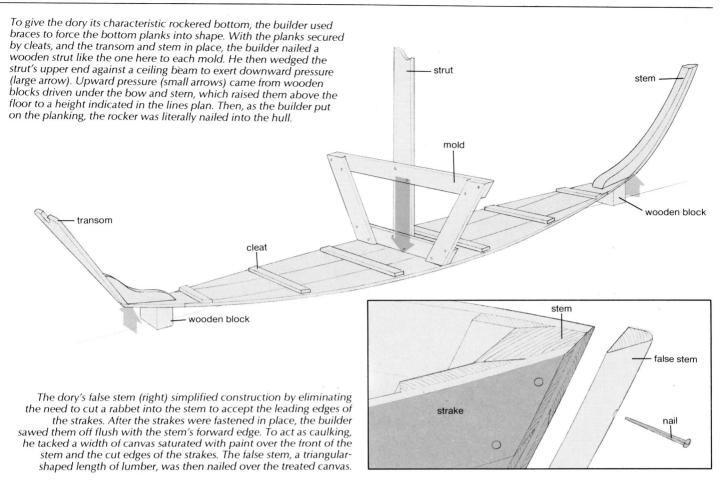

The dory's false stem (right) simplified construction by eliminating the need to cut a rabbet into the stem to accept the leading edges of the strakes. After the strakes were fastened in place, the builder sawed them off flush with the stem's forward edge. To act as caulking, he tacked a width of canvas saturated with paint over the front of the stem and the cut edges of the strakes. The false stem, a triangular-shaped length of lumber, was then nailed over the treated canvas.

A cutaway view of a Grand Banks dory reveals some of its key construction features. Each frame consists of two pieces of wood, one that runs across the boat's bottom and another that sits against the lapstraked side planking; the pieces are joined at the chine with a metal clip, as seen in the cutaway. The removable thwarts are notched to slip over the frames, which hold them in position. Wooden thole pins serve as rudimentary and inexpensive oarlocks, and a notch in the transom receives an oar for steering or sculling.

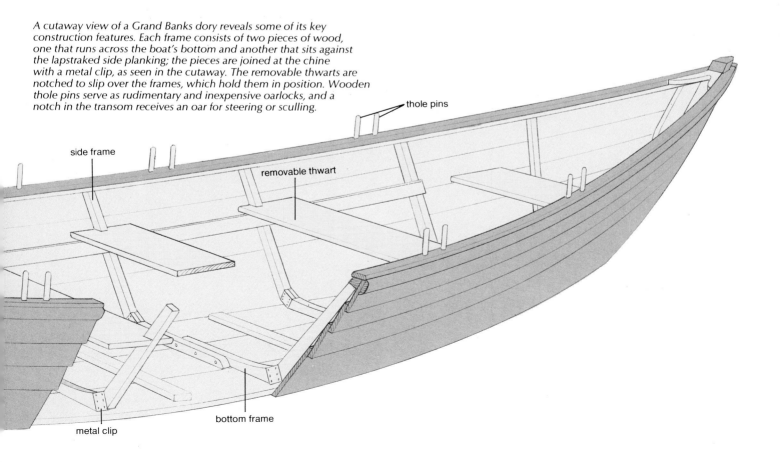

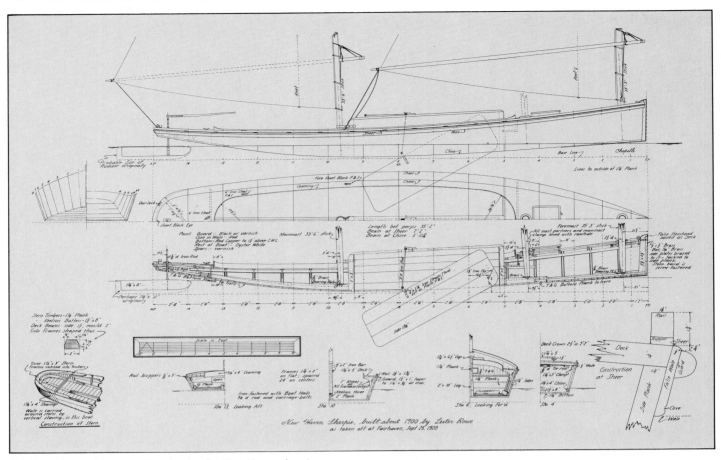

The lines plan and construction plan for the New Haven sharpie
reveal its shallow 1-foot draft and the enormous capacity of its open
cockpit. The profile views show the boat's unique 5-foot reversible
rudder, which could be swung around to tuck under the upswept
stern when oystermen worked off the aft deck. The details at bottom
include a view of the rounded stern at left, and at right the false
wale, which is a thin plank running along the sheer line that protects
the sheer strake and seals it to the outermost deck plank.

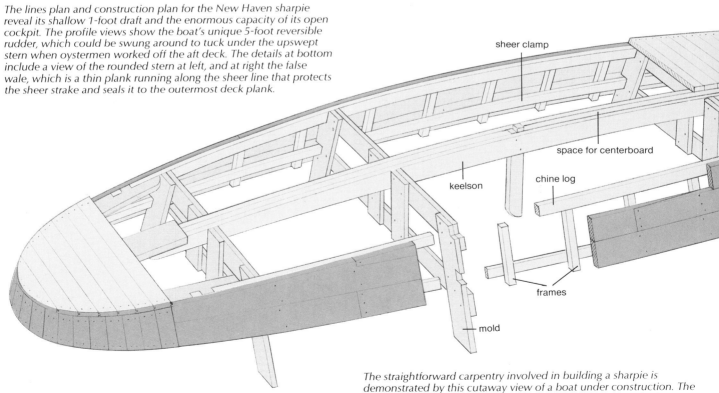

The straightforward carpentry involved in building a sharpie is
demonstrated by this cutaway view of a boat under construction. The
frames for the side planking are simply struts that are attached
between the chine log and sheer clamp. The keelson consists of three
2-by-8-inch planks that run down the center of the hull. A section of
the keelson's middle plank is removed to provide a slot that will
accept the centerboard. The cross planking extends across the hull
bottom and keelson, except at the centerboard opening.

The Sensible Sharpie

In the mid-1870s the oystermen of Long Island Sound evolved a fishing craft ideally suited to their purposes. The New Haven sharpie—25 to 35 feet long, with a flat-bottomed and shallow-draft hull—could carry up to 175 bushels of freshly collected shellfish. Fast and fully seaworthy in relatively protected inshore areas of the Sound, it could be safely handled by a two-man crew. Best of all, it could be built easily and quickly.

Because of its flat, cross-planked bottom, the sharpie needed no elaborate skeleton of ribs and keel. Like many flat-bottomed boats, it was constructed upside down over a set of molds *(below)*. Notches were precut into the molds, into which the builder fitted most of the main structural members, such as the sheer clamps and the keelson. Then he attached some short, simple side frames, and fastened on the carvel side planking. Finally, he put on the bottom planks—sturdy 1¼-inch-thick crosspieces, which provided sufficient structural reinforcement so that bottom framing was not required. Only at the curved stern, which was rounded off, was some fancy carpentry called for *(below, right)*.

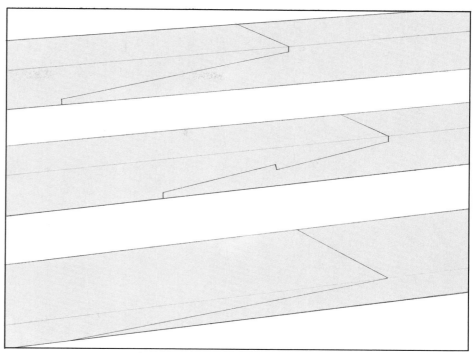

To piece together the sharpie's 35-foot timbers and planks, boatbuilders used a joinery technique called scarphing, three types of which are shown above. In plain scarphing (top), the two pieces were cut at complementary angles and then were screwed or bolted together. Hook scarphing (center) employed an interlocking cut, which protected the joint against pulling apart. In plank scarphing (bottom) the two planks to be joined were cut with tapered or so-called feathered edges, and then were fastened to the frames.

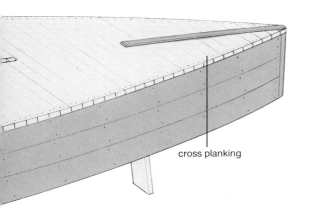

cross planking

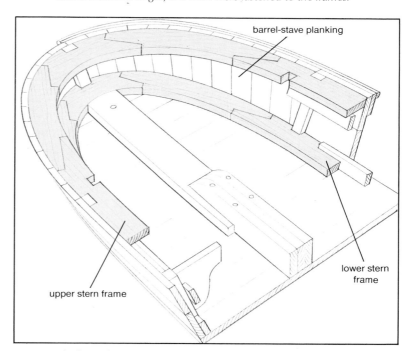

barrel-stave planking

lower stern frame

upper stern frame

The horseshoe curve of the sharpie's stern presented the builder with his most challenging exercise in scarphing. Since no single timber could be bent to such a curve and still keep its strength, both the upper and lower stern pieces, called stern frames, were pieced together from five or more individual sections, each cut so that the grain of the wood conformed as closely as possible to the direction of the curve, and each notched and fitted to its neighbor. The space between the frames was then fitted with vertical barrel-stave planking.

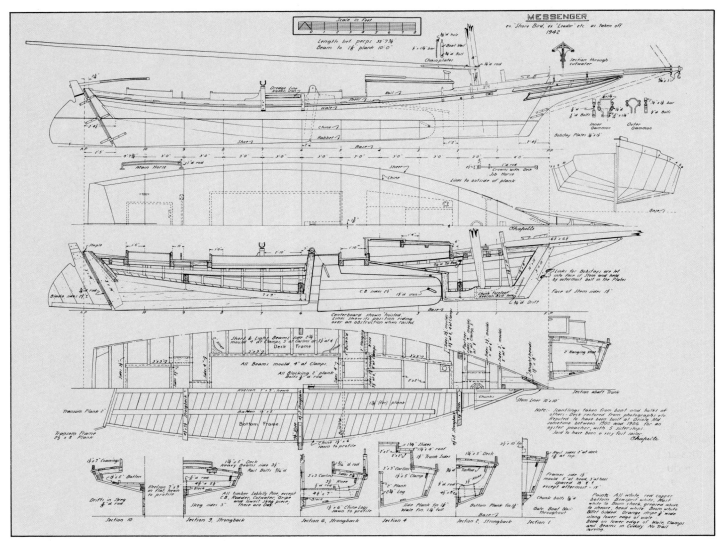

Messenger follows the typical skipjack design, with a solidly constructed, shallow-draft, V-bottom hull, 35 feet long. However, she is slightly trimmer than most skipjacks, for speed in slipping away from government patrol boats. Other skipjack features are the rake of Messenger's transom and mast and her deck arrangement—a cabin forward, a large cargo well amidships and a standing well aft, where a man was able to handle the tiller without having to worry about being hit by a swinging boom. The herringbone pattern of the cross planking on the bottom (lower view) is also common to skipjacks.

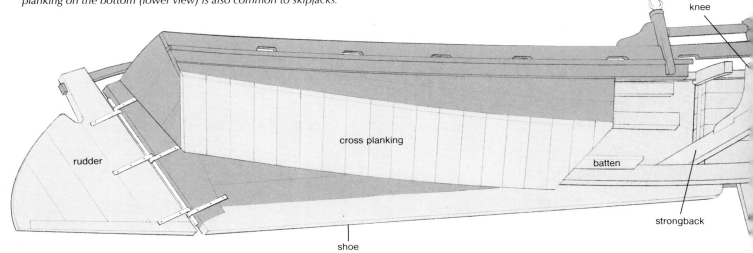

A Chesapeake Legacy

The last of the working sailboats to ply American waters in any significant numbers are the skipjacks of Chesapeake Bay. Close relations of the sharpies, they have been used to dredge oysters from the Chesapeake ever since the turn of the century. The skipjacks' continued use is decreed by state fishery laws; they do far less damage to the oyster beds than would a fleet of modern power dredges. But the skipjacks' durability is also built in—as is evidenced by the massive timbers of the 35-footer, *Messenger*, shown here, constructed to withstand the enormous strain of hauling the oyster dredge in the rough weather of the wintry oyster season.

The skipjack *Messenger* was built in Maryland around 1900 as an oyster pirate —her owner would sail out under cover of night to dredge in areas that were reserved for scooping up the shellfish by hand. Like most oystermen, she has a shallow draft for maneuvering in shoal waters, and a large carrying capacity. Within this basic design, *Messenger* displays a variety of distinguishing skipjack features, developed because of local sailing conditions and design traditions in the Chesapeake area. The most striking of these characteristics are her V-shaped bottom, designed to reduce pounding, and her long bowsprit and enormous clipper bow, borrowed from the fast Baltimore clippers.

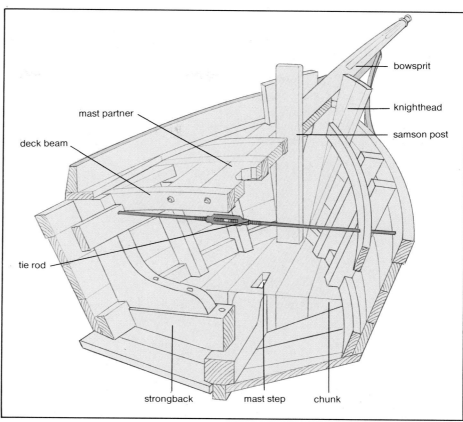

The skipjack's bow reveals extra-solid construction to support the boat's large mast and heavy bowsprit. Five massive pieces called chunks make up the forefoot, and the largest in the center provides a mast step. A samson post, also anchored in the central chunk, rises vertically through the deck to take up the backward thrust of the bowsprit, which is buttressed on either side by a pair of other vertical members—the knightheads. Thick blocks called partners brace the mast. Athwartships, sturdy deck beams, a metal tie rod and a timber strongback reinforce the sides and bottom of the hull.

The skipjack's sturdy construction continues aft, with knees and strongbacks set at intervals along the keelson to brace the hull. Cross planks 1⅜ inches thick are reinforced longitudinally by two battens, five inches wide, and an oak shoe protects the deadwood. Other parts made of white oak are the large centerboard, which is 2½ inches thick, the rudder and the foremost exterior pieces of the bow.

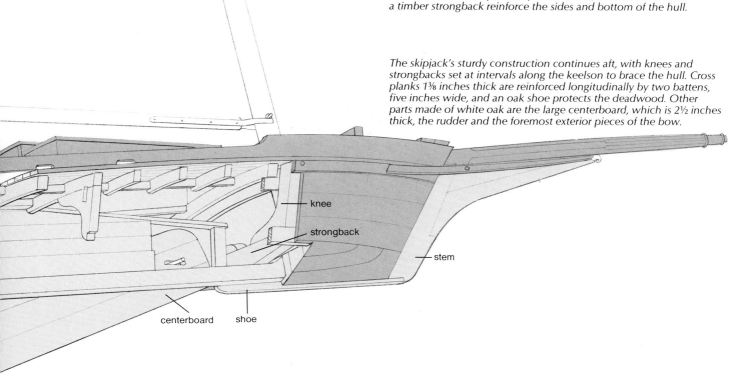

The Elegant Whitehall

The perfect harbor rowboat is quick and easy to the oar, stable and dry in the water, pretty to the eye and roomy enough for one or two passengers or light gear. Just such a craft is the Whitehall, developed in the 1820s as a water taxi and ship chandler's boat in New York Harbor. So appealing was the Whitehall that boats of this type soon appeared in every major American port to ferry passengers and provisions to and from the large ocean-going square-riggers anchored offshore.

The Whitehall derives its popularity from the superb performance of its elegantly curved hull. The hull is 16 to 22 feet long and is fast and easy to handle. Its long waterline gives the Whitehall speed and stability. Its wineglass transom eliminates drag through the water and a deep skeg helps keep the boat on course. Narrow and deep, the bow of the Whitehall cuts through harbor chop, while its flaring sides shed water and keep passengers dry. A gently curving midships section makes the boat roomy and reduces tenderness.

All of this shapeliness exacts a price from the boatbuilder. He must steam-bend each frame to shape, and also must give the frames at the bow and stern an extra twist (opposite, top) to fit them into the hull. And because of the extreme curve taken by the lower few planks (opposite, below), they too need steaming before the builder fastens them in place.

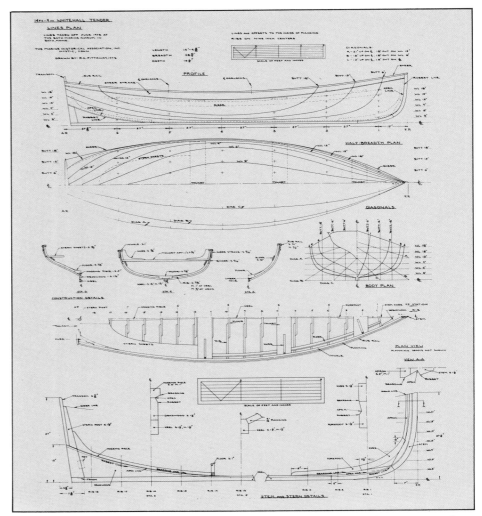

The Whitehall's lines and construction plans present an object lesson in classic elegance and economy of line. Her smoothly curving hull with moderately narrow beam is designed to slip through the water with a minimum of resistance. Her structure is light but strong, with closely spaced frames ⅞ inch thick covered by a skin 9/16 inch thick, once commonly of carvel-planked white cedar.

thwart knee

stern sheets

stern sheets

sheer strake

riser

thwart

floor board

A partially completed Whitehall, shown here in a cutaway view from amidships, has lapped sheer strakes for extra protection of the hull. Horizontal strips called risers run inside the frames to carry the thwarts, and to support the curved seat aft, known as the stern sheets; curved knees brace the thwarts from above. Floor boards provide dry, stable footing for the oarsman and his passengers.

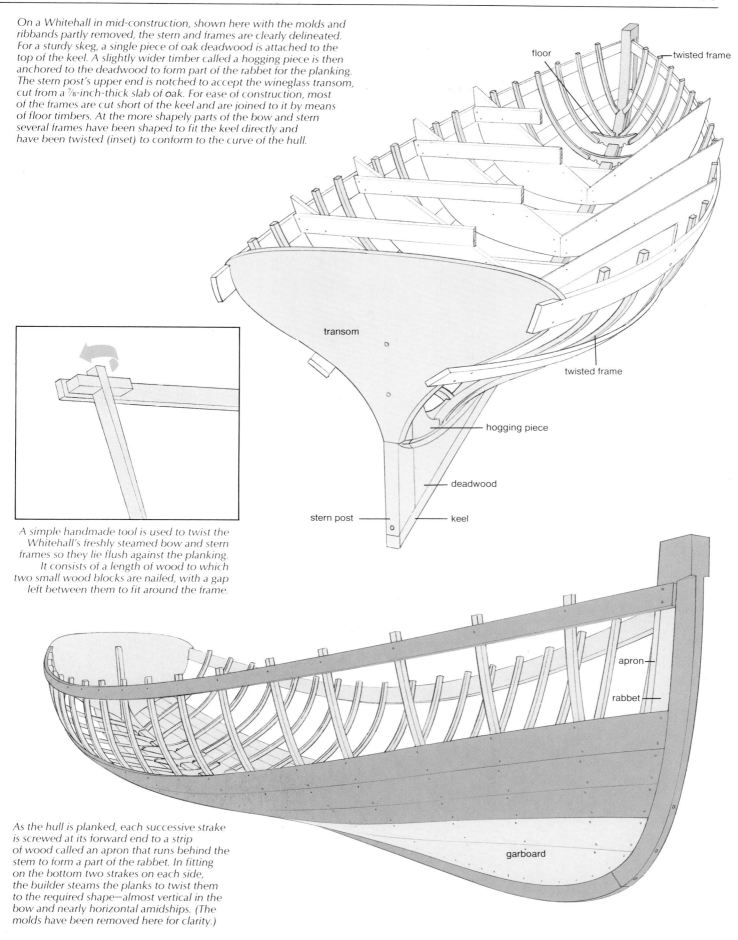

On a Whitehall in mid-construction, shown here with the molds and ribbands partly removed, the stern and frames are clearly delineated. For a sturdy skeg, a single piece of oak deadwood is attached to the top of the keel. A slightly wider timber called a hogging piece is then anchored to the deadwood to form part of the rabbet for the planking. The stern post's upper end is notched to accept the wineglass transom, cut from a 7/8-inch-thick slab of oak. For ease of construction, most of the frames are cut short of the keel and are joined to it by means of floor timbers. At the more shapely parts of the bow and stern several frames have been shaped to fit the keel directly and have been twisted (inset) to conform to the curve of the hull.

floor

twisted frame

transom

twisted frame

hogging piece

deadwood

stern post

keel

A simple handmade tool is used to twist the Whitehall's freshly steamed bow and stern frames so they lie flush against the planking. It consists of a length of wood to which two small wood blocks are nailed, with a gap left between them to fit around the frame.

apron

rabbet

garboard

As the hull is planked, each successive strake is screwed at its forward end to a strip of wood called an apron that runs behind the stem to form a part of the rabbet. In fitting on the bottom two strakes on each side, the builder steams the planks to twist them to the required shape—almost vertical in the bow and nearly horizontal amidships. (The molds have been removed here for clarity.)

The combination lines and construction plan
for the sailing Sea Bright skiff at right show
the shape of a perfect beach boat, even when
converted to motor (opposite, below).
The rounded bow and flat bottom present a
profile with no encumberances to foil a
smooth beaching. The large, deep rudder
detaches for beachings, while the centerboard
retracts fully. The 23-foot hull is beamy
enough at six feet amidships for stability, long
enough to ride the Atlantic rollers, yet
compact enough to be handled by one man.

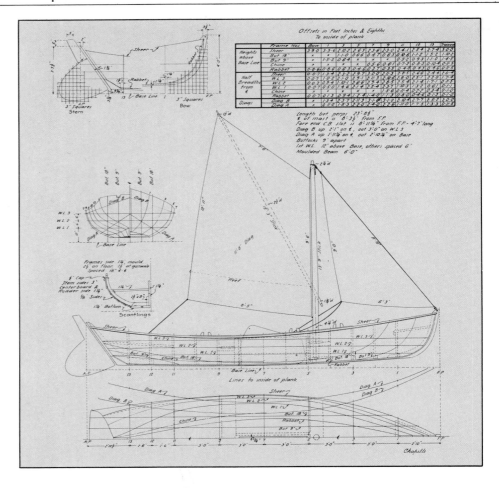

For lightness, strength and resiliency in the pounding surf of the New
Jersey shore, the sailing Sea Bright skiff is lapstraked with buoyant
cedar. Thick sawn oak frames placed 18 inches apart reinforce the
sides of this boat, as seen in the cutaway drawing below. The box in
the aft section of the lower hull is formed when the garboard strake is
twisted until it is almost perpendicular to the flat bottom planks. The
interior of the box creates an easily accessible bilge that
the helmsman can bail out by himself. The helmsman is also aided by
another construction feature, a generous-sized rudder for
steering a cumbersome hull in the tricky ocean tides and currents.

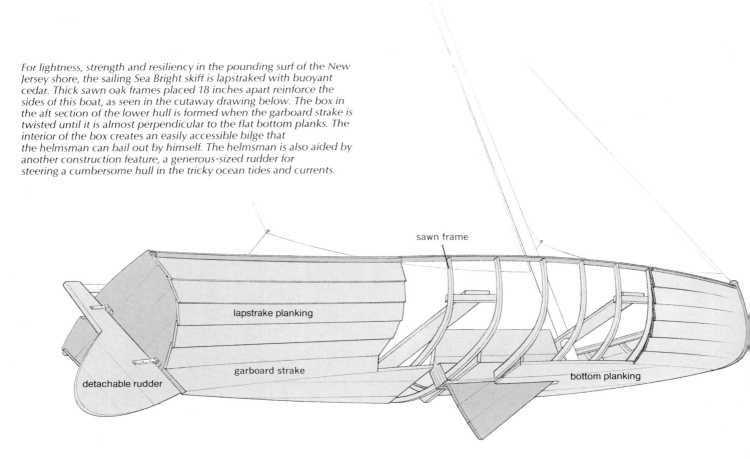

sawn frame

lapstrake planking

garboard strake

bottom planking

detachable rudder

A Skiff for All Times

Around the turn of the century, fishermen began replacing the sails and spars on their workboats with gasoline engines. One boat that adapted particularly well to this transformation was the Sea Bright skiff, which had evolved along the New Jersey coast in the 1850s as a light, relatively dry, and durable fishing craft that could be launched from the beach.

The Sea Bright skiff has a hull reminiscent of the dory's, with rounded, lap-straked sides and a flat bottom of planks running fore and aft. Unlike the dory, the skiff has a garboard strake and flat bottom that form a hollow wooden box in the aft portion of the hull. This box acts like a skeg to stabilize direction when sailing and also prevents the hull from tipping over when the boat is beached.

While the box is a drag that can reduce sailing speeds by up to 25 per cent, it made conversion to power simple. With the engine mounted on the flat bottom, the propeller shaft could go through the end of the box into the water. During Prohibition in the 1920s, the speedy Sea Bright was often used for running whiskey into New York Harbor. A fully loaded 42-foot Sea Bright could outdistance most patrol boats at a speed of 22 knots.

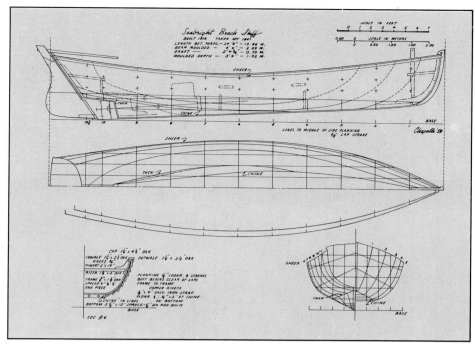

When adapted as a motor boat, the Sea Bright skiff retains its basic profile although it undergoes some construction changes, as seen in its plan. This boat is 35 feet long, one third longer than its sailing counterpart (opposite). With this added length comes more freeboard. The box in the lower hull is also deeper and shorter to create space for the propeller, and the rudder is reduced in size and made permanent. Since it does not extend below the boat, it does not need to be unshipped when the hull is landed on the beach.

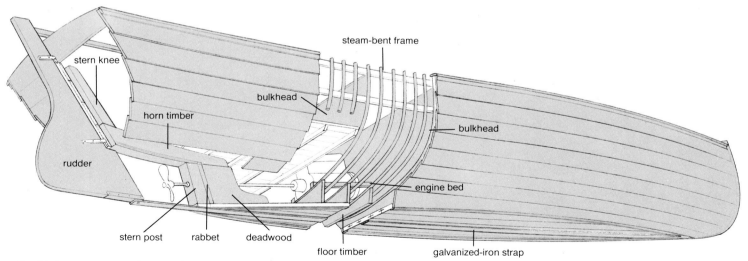

On this longer, motorized Sea Bright skiff the steam-bent oak frames are set only six inches apart, a reinforcement that is relatively light and helps the hull absorb the vibrations of an 11-knot cruising speed. The frames attach to short floor timbers that are set in the box and anchor the frames to the bottom. The engine is mounted on a bed set over the box, and two bulkheads provide an engine compartment. Added support to the stern comes from the stern post, deadwood set in front of it, a horn timber to support the counter over the propeller and a stern knee. A galvanized-iron strap runs between the propeller post and rudder as a bearing for the rudder and a shield for the propeller. Three more straps protect the bottom of the boat.

THE LEONARDO OF EARLY YACHTING

Herreshoff at 77, wearing beard and Panama hat, discusses with client Frank P. Draper a modification to his 60-foot sloop Flying Cloud. Constructed in 1911, Flying Cloud was still in service through the mid-1950s.

Among all the artists and craftsmen who turned head and hand to boatbuilding, none was ever a match for Nathanael Greene Herreshoff, the most talented, versatile and inventive creator of yachts in America and very likely the world. Born in 1848 in the seaport town of Bristol, Rhode Island, on Narragansett Bay, Herreshoff had built and raced his own winning sailing craft by age 10. At 11 he was taking sections off half models and laying down lines for his blind older brother, J.B., who had a small shipbuilding business in town. At 18, he entered M.I.T. to study engineering, and in 1878, young Herreshoff joined J.B. in partnership, taking over as the firm's chief designer.

For the next 56 years he exercised a degree of creative control unprecedented among boatbuilders. Hull, sails, spars, engines, hardware all came under the careful scrutiny of this indefatigably fussy genius, who was always ready to try something new—and usually better. With a sculptor's instinct, he created the shapes of his boats by carving half models freehand, with none of the agonizing mathematics that other designers relied on. And woe betide the customer who questioned those virgin lines. Herreshoff once declined a commission from Kaiser Wilhelm when the Kaiser's representative presumed to suggest some changes.

Other customers, who numbered in the thousands, simply took what the master bestowed—and joyfully. The craft that Herreshoff launched from his Bristol yard ranged from 12-foot day sailers to 145-foot steam yachts, and included the American Navy's first torpedo boat. But his greatest fame came from his racing sailboats—the ultimate measure of a marine architect's artistry and skill. Five America's Cup winners took shape under his hand and eye, including the 144-foot *Reliance*, the largest sloop ever built. And when he died at age 90, the boats created down to the last screw and cringle by the wizard of Bristol had won more races than those of all other designers and builders combined.

A Herreshoff racing sloop of the New York Fifty class gets its double planking laid in the family boatyard's north shop. The Fifty's lightweight hull, trussed at critical stress points with crossed bronze straps that ran between the planking and the frames, held an unusually deep, heavy keel to balance an oversized flight of canvas.

Half models, carved by Herreshoff as the working miniatures of future yachts, line the walls of the master's workshop atop his house on Bristol Harbor, Rhode Island. Herreshoff relied heavily on intuition—and awesome technical skill—for his successful hull designs. From a preliminary sketch, he would fashion a half model out of soft white pine, then sand and shellac it. He used a measuring instrument of his own devising to take down the model's offsets. He would list these in a book, which he gave to the shop as instructions for building the future yacht.

Expert shipwrights in the Herreshoff Manufacturing Company's small-boat shop stand amid boats in progress—all made of wood, which Herreshoff regarded as the only proper substance for the fashioning of small craft. The sloop at the rear is the 26-foot keel-centerboarder Alerion, which Herreshoff designed in 1912 for his own use in Bermuda. The dinghy taking shape in the molds at left will be Alerion's tender, designed with a rocker bottom, a heart-shaped transom and graceful sheer to complement the lines of the mother craft. The boat in the foreground is a lapstrake tender for a larger vessel.

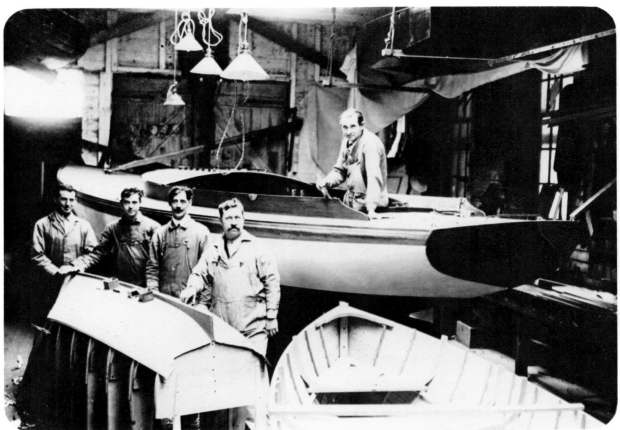

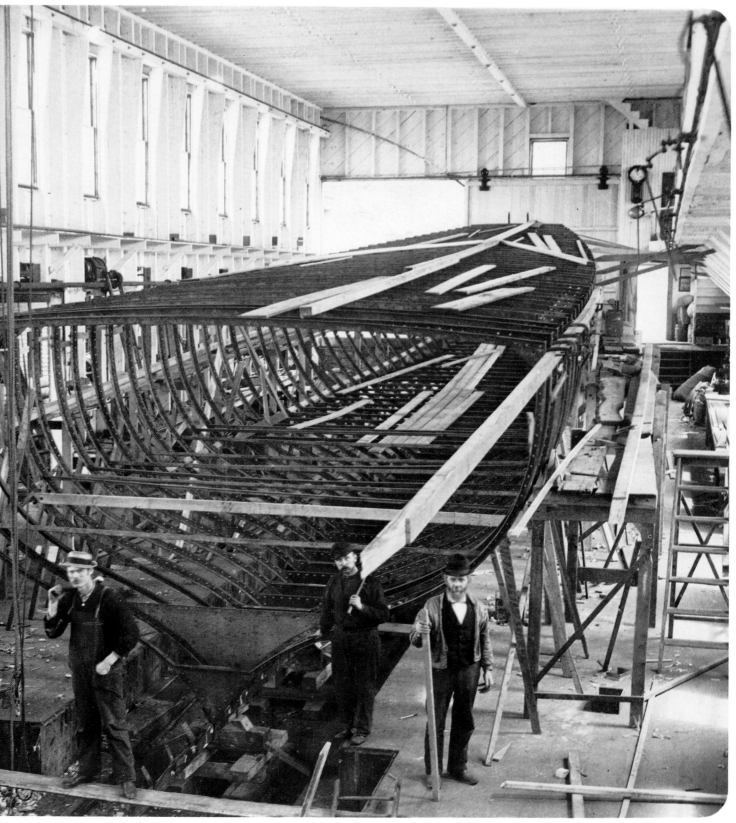

Metalworkers pause while building a large
steam yacht of steel—Herreshoff's preferred
material for vessels over 100 feet. Each metal
section was prefabricated in the firm's
blacksmith shop. The parts were bolted
together on the boat shop floor, then raised,
and held in position by temporary bracing.

A New Cut for Canvas

Not content with turning out the fastest, most graceful hulls of his day, the Bristol master bent his energetic talents to designing and stitching the sails to make them go. He revised the shapes of mainsails and jibs, heightening the rig to take advantage of the extra stability offered by his deep ballast keels. He also ordered an about-face in the way the canvas in his mainsails was pieced together.

For centuries sailmakers had cut mainsails with the cloth panels parallel to the leech. Herreshoff noticed that this construction caused the sails to stretch badly in the wind, and as a result, become less efficient. If the panels were turned to run perpendicular to the leech, Herreshoff reasoned, a sail would hold up better, the wind would flow over it more smoothly and the boat would run faster.

With this flash of common sense, today's crosscut mainsails were born. Herreshoff set up his own sail loft in Bristol and started turning out the new designs. By 1945, when the picture opposite was taken, every racing boat in America was flying a crosscut mainsail.

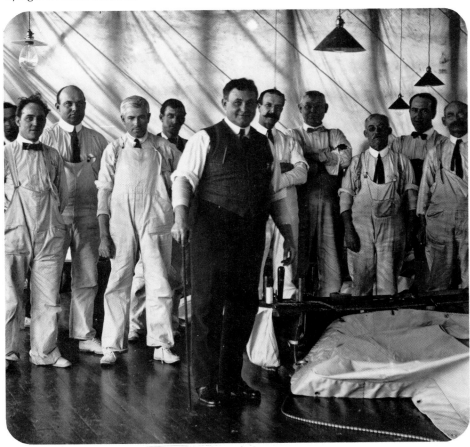

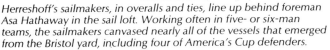
Herreshoff's sailmakers, in overalls and ties, line up behind foreman Asa Hathaway in the sail loft. Working often in five- or six-man teams, the sailmakers canvased nearly all of the vessels that emerged from the Bristol yard, including four of America's Cup defenders.

With crosscut mainsails taut and full of wind, a fleet of Herreshoff S-boats sprints toward the start of a race on Narragansett Bay. Introduced in 1919, the S-boats were one of Herreshoff's most popular designs, and he manufactured every component aboard.

Metalwork Innovations

Nearly half the buildings at the Bristol yard were devoted to metalworking operations such as blacksmithing and machine assembling. For Herreshoff put his stamp not only upon hull design and sails, but also upon every other aspect of a boat's production. He would often build an entire engine to the requirements of an individual yacht. A perfectionist in small items as well as large, he forged his own cleats, winches, anchors and propellers *(overleaf)*, in designs that set new standards for the marine-hardware industry.

One celebrated Herreshoff invention was the sail track, which allowed a closer marriage of sail and mast than was possible with the (wooden) hoops then generally used. And since the mast did not have to be kept clear for the hoops, it could be braced with spreaders, permitting lighter and taller spars.

Herreshoff's improved variation of the belaying cleat has lengthened horns, tapered at the ends and waist, to carry more turns of rope than the earlier models. Of hollow-cast bronze, it also features widely spaced feet with four bolt holes rather than two, for greater stability and strength.

The yard's machine shop produced a generation of ultralight, mechanically innovative steam engines, whose parts were produced in this room or in the adjoining foundry. Not surprisingly, the energy to drive the machines came from a Herreshoff steam engine.

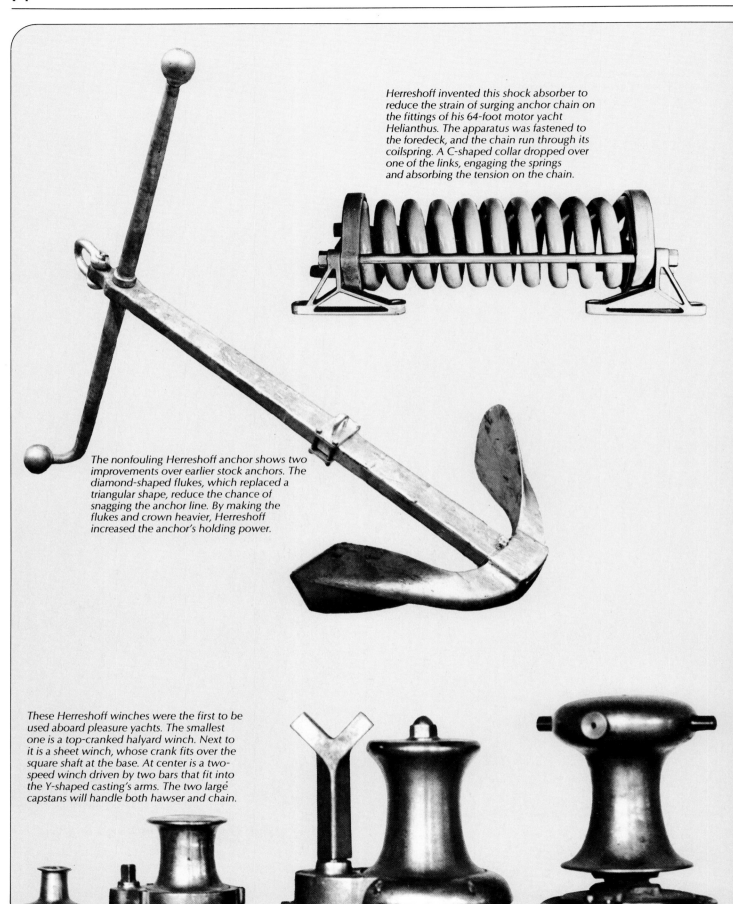

Herreshoff invented this shock absorber to reduce the strain of surging anchor chain on the fittings of his 64-foot motor yacht Helianthus. The apparatus was fastened to the foredeck, and the chain run through its coilspring. A C-shaped collar dropped over one of the links, engaging the springs and absorbing the tension on the chain.

The nonfouling Herreshoff anchor shows two improvements over earlier stock anchors. The diamond-shaped flukes, which replaced a triangular shape, reduce the chance of snagging the anchor line. By making the flukes and crown heavier, Herreshoff increased the anchor's holding power.

These Herreshoff winches were the first to be used aboard pleasure yachts. The smallest one is a top-cranked halyard winch. Next to it is a sheet winch, whose crank fits over the square shaft at the base. At center is a two-speed winch driven by two bars that fit into the Y-shaped casting's arms. The two large capstans will handle both hawser and chain.

America's earliest folding propeller came out of Herreshoff's metal shop in 1910. The turning of the prop shaft under power produced enough centrifugal force to open the blades (top). When the shaft stopped turning, the propeller closed (bottom).

The Bristol master designed this five-cylinder steam engine for the U.S. Navy's first seagoing torpedo boat, the U.S.S. Cushing. To shorten the crankshaft and lighten the engine, he repositioned the valve gear drives and specified hollow steel parts. Both innovations would later be adopted for gasoline engines by the auto industry.

Reliance under sail slices through a calm sea off Newport, Rhode Island, where that summer she would meet Sir Thomas Lipton's Shamrock III. In earning the right to defend the Cup, and later against Shamrock, she never lost a race. She carried 16,160 square feet of sail and required an afterguard and crew of 64, despite a battery of winches to work many of the sheets and halyards. Her topsail, housed on a telescoping topmast that could be raised and lowered through the hollow steel mast, is larger than the mainsails of today's 12-meter sloops. There has never been a yacht to match her.

The majestic stern of the 1903 America's Cup defender Reliance, the master's masterpiece and the most majestic sloop ever built, emerges from the south shop of the Bristol yard. Commissioned by a New York Yacht Club syndicate at a cost of about $175,000, she measured 90 feet on the waterline, as specified by the rule then governing Cup races. But when fully rigged she stretched more than 200 feet from the tip of her bowsprit to the end of her boom.

3 Building a new boat is a straightforward business. It proceeds with a certain logic from the drawing of the plans right through to the launching of the vessel, and it follows a fairly predictable timetable. But restoring an old boat is full of. uncertainties and can often entail more work and more cost than starting from scratch, as Jarvis Newman, owner of *Dictator,* opposite, discovered in the process of bringing the 70-odd-year-old sloop back to life.

Newman, who is by trade a builder of fiberglass boats in Southwest Harbor, Maine, found his prize during a chance visit to a boatyard in nearby Stonington, Deer Isle. *Dictator,* 31 feet long, was cradled at the yard, a gaping

DICTATOR: SAGA OF RESTORATION

hole in her starboard bow where some planks had been lifted, and she looked forlorn indeed. Newman was nonetheless smitten instantly. Not only was *Dictator* a Friendship sloop, a clipper-bowed fisherman's classic, long celebrated in Maine for her graceful lines and seakindliness, but she was a McLain Friendship; she had been built by Robert E. McLain, whom some marine historians consider the originator of the Friendship sloop. Jarvis Newman could see Mc-Lain's sure hand in *Dictator's* uncommonly beautiful sheer line, in her huge, rounded cockpit, in her small, shallow cabin which so subtly enhanced the sleek, low profile of the sloop. A closer inspection of the hull, revealing *Dictator's* internal injuries—rotten frames, a cutwater gone, iron fastenings rusted away—did nothing to dampen the visitor's ardor. He bought the sloop, knowing he would have to replace virtually every stick and fitting on her.

Owner Newman set himself three fundamental criteria for the project. First, he wanted to stay as close as was practicable to McLain's original design, materials and workmanship so that the sloop when finished would truly be a restoration of *Dictator* and not *Dictator II.* Second, he wanted a boat that would, within these limitations, be suitable for family sailing—that is, comfortable and easy to handle. Last, *Dictator* would not have to measure up to museum standards of authenticity; where better materials or better ideas were available, Newman was fully prepared to bend the rules. Traditional iron fastenings would be ruled out in favor of bronze, and extra strength would be built into the notoriously weak Friendship deck and flooring. He would replace the rock ballasting with a lead keel, have sails cut along modern lines from lightweight modern cloth, and install an engine for auxiliary power. He would also design a snug cabin, equipped for overnight cruising, in place of Mc-Lain's basic working cabin, and add such refinements as a bronze eagle billethead, and a pair of kerosene running lights housed in polished brass. Newman felt comfortable in the conviction that McLain, a sensible man, would have done the same given the circumstances.

With his plans thought through, and *Dictator* moved to his own boatyard, Newman began the actual labor. To recapture *Dictator's* original lines, he went to the hull itself. Working backward from the damaged timbers, he developed a set of lines plans—McLain had presumably worked from a half model in the manner of most oldtime boatbuilders. These new plans, plus the hull parts Newman painstakingly disassembled, became his principal teachers. He also had the help of his friend, Ralph Stanley, a boatbuilder far more experienced than he in the fine points of wood construction.

The restoration effort took Newman, by his own careful accounts, 2,805 man-hours and close to $35,000, but it was a rich learning experience, both professionally and personally. Three years after he bought the battered sloop, *Dictator* was ready to join her sister Friendships on Maine's Muscongus Bay. She quickly captured a number of prizes for her performance, doing both Jarvis Newman and Robert McLain proud.

The sloop Dictator, restoration well along, shows off her new decks and coaming. The wheel, which replaced Dictator's original tiller years ago, was eventually reinstalled.

Robert E. McLain, Dictator's builder and one of the early developers of the Friendship sloop, is pictured with his wife and son sometime in the 1890s. Mrs. McLain, a sturdy helpmate, made Dictator's first suit of sails at home on her treadle sewing machine.

Genealogy of a Sloop

In the process of securing legal title to his newly discovered sloop, Jarvis Newman made a fascinating research excursion back to 1904 when shipwright Robert E. McLain *(left)* built *Dictator.* McLain lived on an island in Muscongus Bay, Maine. That winter he built two sturdy vessels, keeping one for himself and selling the future *Dictator* to lobsterman Stephen Grey. For six years Grey found her to be not only a fine boat but fortuitously inexpensive: the bank from which he had borrowed the $300 purchase price failed before he had paid off his debt.

In 1910 Grey sold the sloop to another lobsterman, Roy W. Sargent, who moored her in a small cove on the mainland. Three years later Sargent, in turn, sold the boat to a Fred Torrey, who used *Dictator* for herring and mackerel fishing. Then, after 10 more years, title passed to William Raynes, a ferryman in the islands around Mount Desert. Raynes soon sold the sloop to Dr. Alan Chesney, a summer vacationer, and she remained a family pleasure boat for the next 46 years.

Dictator, like all early Friendships, was continually being changed and rebuilt. Grey, for example, put in an engine. Torrey removed it. Raynes changed *Dictator's* rig, replacing her jib and forestaysail with a single larger jib, and substituted a wheel for her original tiller. The Chesneys replaced three masts and two bowsprits, and they added dozens of reinforcing ribs to her aging hull.

During these years the sloop had a number of narrow escapes. An overheated engine set its mount afire in the 1920s, but the blaze was extinguished. A storm in the '30s broke her loose from her mooring, but she fetched up on a sloping sand beach. Though essentially undamaged by these mishaps, years of weathering and wear had taken a steady toll. By the time Newman bought *Dictator* in 1971, the heel ends of many of her ribs were rotted out, necessitating a major overhaul.

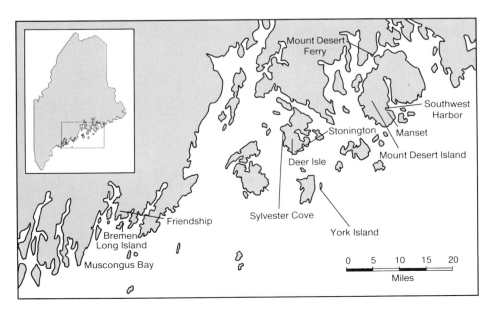

In over 70 years Dictator never has gone far from Bremen Long Island, where she was launched. Original owner Stephen Grey lived in Stonington, on Deer Isle, and lobstered off York Island. Roy Sargent sailed her out of Mount Desert Ferry, and Fred Torrey fished out of Manset. Next, she stayed at Manset with William Raynes—until the Chesneys took her to Deer Isle's Sylvester Cove. Newman brought her to Southwest Harbor.

Third owner Fred Torrey coils the halyards as Dictator slides away from the dock. When this photograph was taken, around 1920, she still boasted a double-headsail rig— although only the forestaysail is set here.

One of the Chesney clan takes Dictator out for passage around Bass Harbor Head, Mount Desert, in 1947. Though the rig had been altered to one foresail, and the original sails long since replaced, the sloop still carried the traditional vertically cut sails.

A Perilous Passage

Having traced *Dictator*'s lineage until he was able to sign bona fide ownership papers, Jarvis Newman was faced with the demanding task of having the battered and disintegrating old craft moved from Francis Williams' boatyard in Stonington on Deer Isle, where her previous owners, the Chesneys, had left her, to his own yard at Southwest Harbor. Before abandoning *Dictator*, the Chesneys had her carefully cradled, thus preserving the basic hull shape. But otherwise, she was a shambles.

Her decks and ceilings were masses of rot. The portside garboard was missing from the stem to amidships. Most disheartening was the gaping hole in her starboard bow *(see below)*, put there on her last voyage by a relative of the Chesneys. *Dictator* could have been trucked overland from Stonington to Southwest Harbor. But the 35-mile trip would be costly and difficult—as a matter of fact, the twisting, bumpy local roads might shake the craft's fragile hull to pieces.

Newman and Williams decided instead to have the boat towed across by water. Newman returned to Southwest Harbor to prepare a cradle for her, and Williams set about making her hull as watertight as possible. Planks were nailed across all the gaps on the hull, and a heavy canvas cover bandaged her bow. Then *Dictator* was gingerly slipped into the water, with her spars tied across her deck. As added insurance, four blocks of Styrofoam flotation were slipped beneath her cockpit floor.

On a frigid November morning, Newman, boatyard owner Williams and a helper set off for Southwest Harbor. Their voyage was a short one; *Dictator* started sinking barely two miles from the dock, and she was almost underwater before they got her back to Williams' boatyard. There they hastily stripped the boat of her heavy spars (which were later shipped to Southwest Harbor by truck), and with *Dictator* riding higher, they set out several days later for Southwest Harbor.

This time *Dictator* and her crew made it, but just barely. The hour was 2 p.m.; even with a powerful motor-driven ditch pump going, the boat was foundering. It seemed impossible for Newman to get *Dictator* safely into a cradle.

They had no choice but to wait for high water, which would not come until early morning. Snow began to fall. At 5 a.m., in a driving snowstorm, *Dictator* floated again. Using a workboat, Newman guided her into her cradle. Then with a tractor, he dragged *Dictator*, in her cradle, up a ramp and into a field beside his workshop.

Her new owner Jarvis Newman took this photograph of the rotting, rust-streaked Dictator in Stonington, as he found her, just before he had the hulk towed to Southwest Harbor. A good cradling job by the boatyard owner preserved her essential lines. The heavy crosspieces beneath her keel distributed Dictator's weight, and kept her keel from sagging. Minimal side bracing cut the risk of her sides being pushed in.

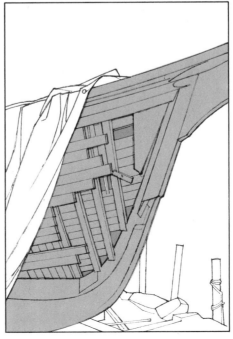

Dictator's battered bow shows a latticework of exposed hull timbers and sawed-off planks. But the cutwater is missing, and so is a substantial area of planking. A few frames and ceilings are virtually all that holds the bow together. The planks were sawed away in 1969, in preparation for repairs that were never made on her stove-in bow section.

Leaking and listing, Dictator floats with waterline submerged just after her arrival at a dock in Southwest Harbor. The canvas patch over her bow helped her survive the trip from Stonington. The gasoline-powered pump on her deck proved of little use against the water that kept pouring through her as she waited to be put into her cradle. The small cabin trunk and the fully rounded cockpit coaming are rare among Friendship sloops. Most of them had longer cabins and smaller cockpits.

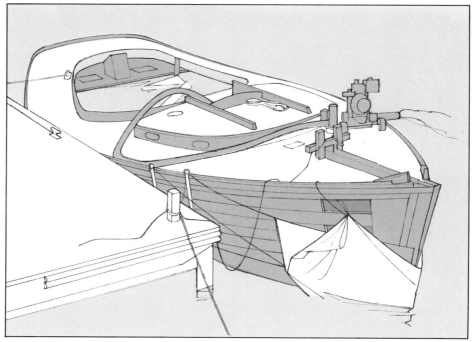

Preserving the Shape

Before any restoration could be done, Newman had to have the most accurate record possible of the original hull shape. Since McLain built from a model and there were no plans, he took the lines off the boat itself. The first step was to set the hull's waterline absolutely level, to establish a constant reference for a plumb line to be used in making offsets. Next he laid down the center line as another reference, and then divided the length of the hull into equal sections—or stations. Finally, *Dictator's* lines were taken off at each station, and her offsets noted down.

Newman took the lines from the starboard side of *Dictator's* hull. Then, when drawing up the actual lines plan, he noted where the hull had been repaired, or obviously bent out of shape by years of use, and faired the lines in order to keep a smooth and flowing shape.

To make sure that Dictator's hull lies level, a transparent hose partly filled with water was draped over the bow and stern, as shown. Since the water at both ends of a hose will rise to exactly the same height, Newman was able to level the waterline of Dictator's hull by matching its alignment with the water in the hose. The entire leveling process took three hours, during which the men jacked and shimmed the cradle until the boat's waterline was perfectly horizontal.

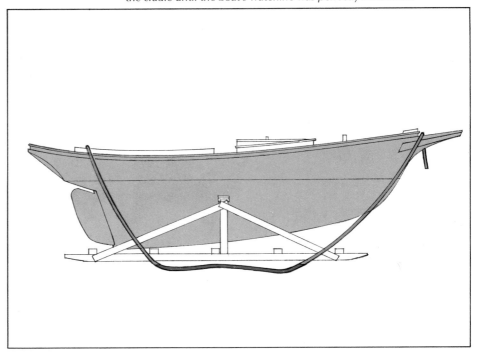

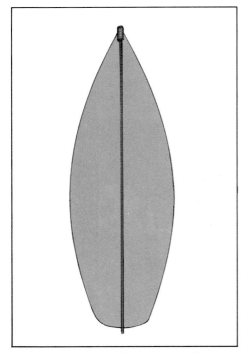

With the waterline set level, Newman laid down a center line by stringing a length of twine along the deck from the middle of the transom to the stem. Next, he fixed stations along the center line, and then made a series of measurements outward from the line and perpendicular to it, to determine the exact shape of the hull's half-breadth, or plan view.

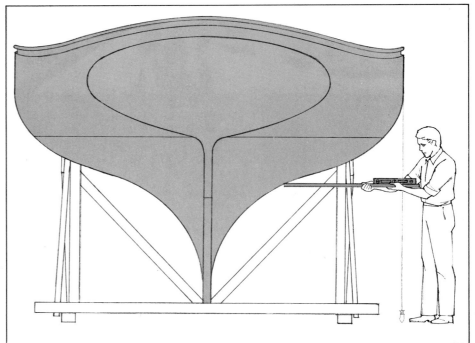

To get the offsets for the buttock lines, Newman hung a plumb line from a nail driven in at each station just below the deck edge and then used a ruler and a level to measure the perpendicular distance from the plumb line to a series of points on the side of the hull. As many as a dozen points were measured, both above and below the waterline, at every station. Finally, the hundreds of points that resulted from these measurements and the half-breadth were plotted on paper and joined together to form Dictator's lines plan.

The completed lines for Dictator (top and center, below) show the beautiful sheer line typical of a Friendship sloop, and the perfect meeting of the transom's point at the high waterline unique to Newman's own craft. The bottom drawing is a skeletal construction plan, delineating the shape of Dictator's projected new backbone.

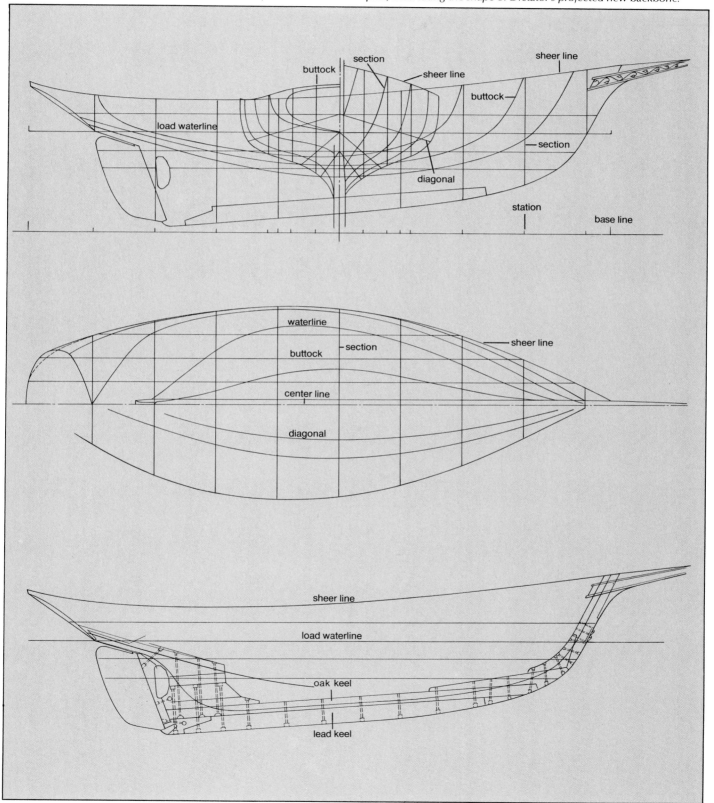

The two ledger pages above record the daily work undertaken from February 23 to July 23. The columns of numbers that follow each project entry register man-hours expended and costs of materials.

Fittings and Accessories

Number and Material	Source				
1 billethead, bronze	Maine	2 gooseneck bands, bronze	Maine	2,000 screws (2" x 12"), bronze	Massachusetts
2 bitts, bronze	Pennsylvania	1 gudgeon, bronze	Maine	5,000 screws (2" x 14"), bronze	Massachusetts
12 blocks, lignum vitae	Nova Scotia	1 mast trunk, lignum vitae	Nova Scotia		
4 chain plates, bronze	Nova Scotia	10 mast hoops, red oak	Massachusetts	300 feet standing rigging wire, stainless steel	Maine
12 cleats, bronze	Connecticut	10 parrel beads, lignum vitae	Nova Scotia	1 stove, cast iron	Nova Scotia
8 deadeyes, lignum vitae	Nova Scotia	4 portholes, bronze	Italy	1 stuffing box, bronze	Connecticut
1 diesel engine, cast iron	England	1 propeller, bronze	Michigan	5 through-hull fittings, bronze	Connecticut
1 gaff jaws, red oak	Massachusetts	1 propeller shaft, bronze	Maine		
1 gooseneck, bronze	Maine	1 stern bearing, bronze	Maine	2 travelers, bronze	Maine

A Full Accounting

Before Newman began the physical work of reconstructing *Dictator,* he put in long months of careful preparation. With the help of his colleague, Ralph Stanley, he drew up a list *(opposite)* that detailed the types and quantities of wood that would be needed to complete the job. Setting the highest standards of resilience, resistance to rot, and appearance, he chose nine different varieties of wood—some of them too expensive for the original Maine builders, or simply unavailable to them. While cedar was plentiful locally, for example, other types such as the teak for the cabin trim were imported woods that required some searching to locate. One extravagant item on the list—the 12 board feet of rare holly that went into the handsome cabin sole—won a berth on *Dictator* chiefly because the owner had a stock of it on hand in his boatshed.

As the lumber supplies began to arrive from the mills and supply houses, *Dictator's* builder took great care to store each type of wood properly. He received the cedar early in May, and stacked it outdoors in a three-cornered pile so that the wind, sun and rain would season it over the summer. When fall came he restacked the cedar inside a heated, dry shed. He scheduled the delivery of the kiln-dried fir for a dry summer day and stacked it inside immediately, with spacers put between the planks. The oak, which would be steamed and bent later, was ordered green and kept that way by storing it on a cement floor in an unheated shed.

Nearly two years before her launching, Newman also anticipated the fittings *Dictator* would need *(opposite, below).* Many of the items were either custom orders or available only from foreign chandlers, so he needed to leave plenty of advance time in case of delays or mistakes. Finally, he began keeping a ledger *(opposite)* as a permanent record of the sloop's reconstruction. It opened on November first with the matter-of-fact entry "Purchased *Dictator* $1,000." It ended triumphantly on July 28, two years later: "Sat. Race—1st Overall out of 52 sloops."

Wood Ordered for Restoration

Use	Amount	Variety and Source
decking	1,600 feet of 1 $\frac{1}{16}$" x 1 $\frac{1}{2}$", 10 to 14 feet long	Douglas fir from Oregon
deck frames	500 feet of 1 $\frac{1}{16}$" x 3 $\frac{1}{2}$"	
bowsprit	16 feet of 5 $\frac{3}{8}$" x 8"	
planking	1,600 feet of 1 $\frac{1}{8}$" live edge 400 feet of 1 $\frac{1}{4}$" live edge	cedar from Maine
king planks	12 feet of 1 $\frac{1}{16}$" x 8"	
waterways	used leftover cedar from planking	
cabin sides	2 pieces 1" x 12" x 16 feet	white oak from Georgia
coaming	2 pieces 1" x 16" x 16 feet	
ceiling	3,070 feet of $\frac{7}{16}$" x 1 $\frac{1}{4}$"	cypress from Georgia
interior cabinets	20 feet of $\frac{3}{4}$" x 10"	teak from Thailand
outside trim	60 feet of 1"	
interior trim and cabin sole	30 feet of 1" x 12"	
cabin sole	12 board feet	holly already in shop
frames	94 timbers 1 $\frac{1}{8}$" x 2 $\frac{1}{2}$" x 10 feet	red oak from Maine
bilge stringers	4 pieces 1 $\frac{1}{4}$" x 4" x 18 feet	
sheer clamp	4 pieces 1 $\frac{1}{4}$" x 3" x 18 feet	
shelf	4 pieces 1 $\frac{1}{4}$" x 2 $\frac{1}{2}$" x 18 feet	
engine bed, bow bitt and stern frame	2 pieces 4" x 6" x 12 feet	
keel	6" x 7" x 22 feet	
deadwood	3 pieces 7" x 12" x 6 feet	
floor timbers	400 feet of 2" x 12"	
horn timber and shaft log	1 piece 8" x 14" x 12 feet	
forefoot	1 piece 7" x 12" x 6 feet	
stem and stern knees	1 piece 5" x 14" x 12 feet	
boom	1 tree	spruce from Maine
bulkheads	10 sheets 4 feet x 8 feet x $\frac{1}{2}$"	Duraply
main bulkhead	1 sheet 4 feet x 8 feet x $\frac{3}{4}$"	
cabin top	6 sheets 4 feet x 8 feet x $\frac{1}{4}$"	

The New Skeleton

To faithfully preserve *Dictator*'s original lines, Newman and his crew shaped the new frames inside what remained of her 1904 hull; the old hull thus became a template for building a virtually new boat.

The first step was to remove *Dictator*'s rotted backbone, and make room to install a new one. To do this the owner constructed an ingenious cradle *(right)* that supported *Dictator* along her sides without resting any weight on her keel. It then was relatively easy work to saw through each frame at garboard level—permitting *Dictator*'s original backbone to drop out on the workshop floor.

The restorers then began assembling *Dictator*'s new backbone. They cut and shaped a keel from red oak, and bolted on a stem, forefoot, deadwood and horn timber, also of red oak. Then they cut notches, called timber gains, every 18 inches to receive the butt ends of new frames.

Next, the owner and his helpers removed what remained of *Dictator*'s original decking. They also took off every second plank along her sides—creating a mold of sorts to which the new frames could be clamped. The owner made each of these new frames of 1⅛-inch-by-2½-inch oak. For added strength and suppleness, he sliced each frame lengthwise down the center with a bandsaw, leaving only the last 6 inches at the butt end whole. The result was a sturdy, supple, two-ply frame, with one ply resting against the planking, and the other ply on the inward side.

Dictator's owner needed three helpers to put in the frames—one to work a steam box that softened the wood, and two to quickly clamp the frames to the planks. As with the planking, the men at first replaced only every other frame. Then, after checking the work against a lines plan of the vessel, they went back and replaced the frames that remained.

Dictator's massive horn timber, deadwood and keel, viewed from astern, await framing. Both the horn timber and keel have already been notched to receive the frames, and a hole has been bored for the propeller shaft through the shaft log. To affix the keel to the other backbone pieces, the owner set a number of blind bolts—a technique used for joining heavy timbers. To seat the bolt's nut, Newman had to cut a window into the side of the receiving timber. He then slipped the bolt into the bolt hole, secured the nut through the window and plugged it with a tight-fitting wood dowel called a dutchman.

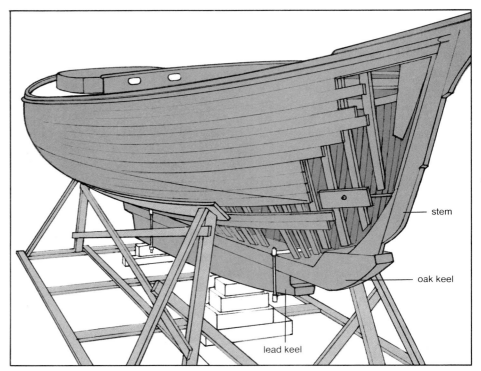

Dictator rests on props that support her hull sides but not her keel. Here, her old keel has been sawed away, leaving the lower ends of her frames and stem exposed. Positioned under her hull, not attached to it, are her new oak keel and a 5,300-pound lead ballast keel.

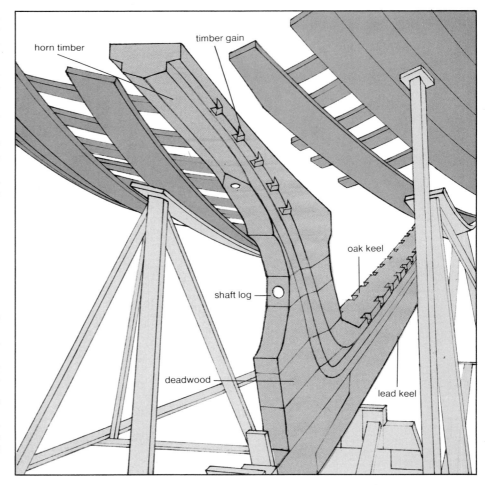

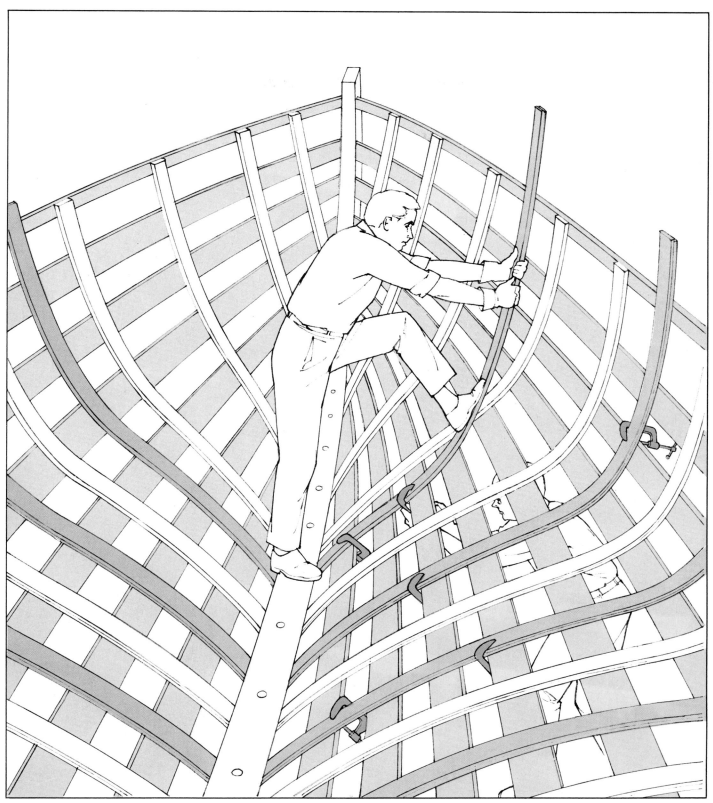

Newman and his helper install a frame, a process that took fast, precise teamwork, since the wood stayed fully pliable for barely 15 seconds after leaving the steam box. With one man stationed inside the hull, the man at the steam box passed each hot frame to him, and he quickly jammed its butt into a timber gain. Then, holding the frame with his gloved hands, he forced it with one foot against Dictator's planking. Outside the hull, two men clamped it to the planking. Finally, they pounded on the exposed head of each frame to make certain that it was fully set into the curvature of the hull.

From Strakes to Floors

With *Dictator's* skeleton completed, Newman and his men began to flesh her out, starting with a complete layer of new cedar hull planking. They worked from the bottom up, taking 14 days to lay the sloop's 17 strakes of planking. In the process, each of the remaining old planks was carefully pried off, and a new plank fastened in place before the next old plank above was removed.

When the planking was completed, two men began to install *Dictator's* oak clamps—those longitudinal timbers that run inside the frames along the main lines of hull stress; one clamp went on at the sheer and one at the turn of the bilge.

Then the restoration team laid in the floor timbers—heavy oak pieces that lock the frames and planking to the backbone. The original *Dictator* had had only three floor timbers—a common structural mistake that had left the hulls of many old-time Friendship sloops too weak. Newman, benefiting from this knowledge, took his first major departure from authenticity: he increased the number of floor timbers to 18. His second departure was in the hull fastenings he used *(right)*.

Using C-clamps and wooden wedges called planking dogs to hold a new plank in place, a workman sets pairs of bronze screws at each intersection of plank and frame. Oldtime Friendship builders saved money and time by using rust-prone galvanized-iron nails.

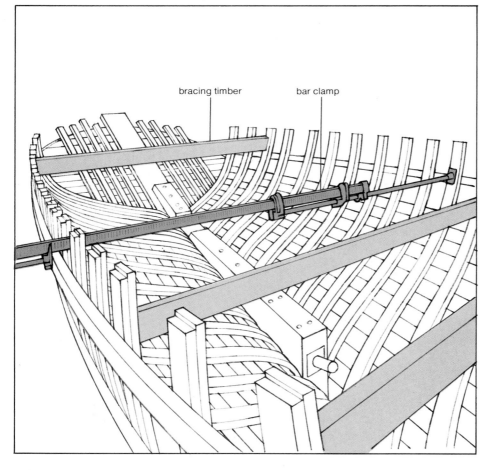

bracing timber   bar clamp

Hefty athwartship timbers and adjustable steel bar clamps provide temporary interior bracing for the undecked hull during the planking operation. After the last plank was screwed on, the bracing was replaced by a framework of crossbeams and longitudinal timbers that both completed the boat's hull structure and supported the deck.

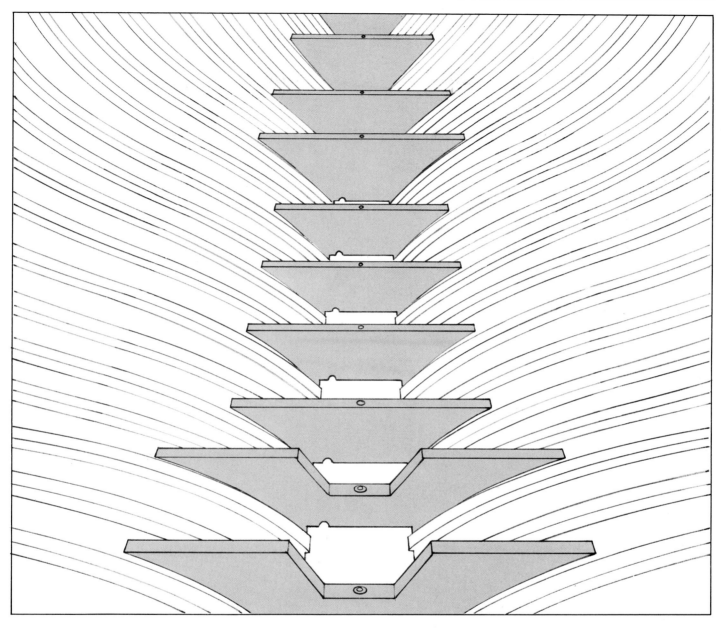

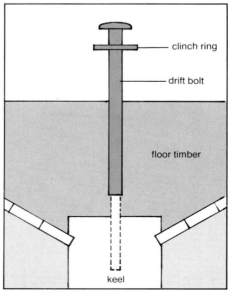

To marry the hull even more precisely to the backbone, Dictator's new owner set floor timbers between every other pair of frames, notching two timbers near the stern to make space for an engine. Following a procedure common on Friendships, Newman also attached the floor timbers to the planks, setting screws through the planks and the timbers from outside the hull. He used a single drift bolt (right) to fix each floor timber to the keel as well.

clinch ring

drift bolt

floor timber

keel

A drift bolt is poised in its hole in a floor timber before being driven down into the keel. Newman cut his drift bolts to the desired lengths from a ½-inch bronze rod; he then tapered one end so that it would drive into the wood more easily. Next, he drilled a hole into each floor timber, using a bit slightly smaller than the rod's diameter. Then he positioned the bolt point down, slipped a washer called a clinch ring over it and drove the bolt home. The top of the rod had been broadened out into a rough bolthead beforehand and now set snug against the clinch ring.

Once the owner had installed the deck framing, he laid up the inner skin or ceiling—the task in progress here. Almost simultaneously, he began work on the cabin sides and cockpit coaming—parts of which had already been steamed, clamped in place above the deck framing, and drilled to receive ¼-inch countersunk bronze bolts. He also positioned the king plank in the bow and cut the mast partners. Belowdecks he painted Dictator's bilges with red lead and bedded her engine, a diesel with a fiberglass drip tray to catch oil waste.

A Stronger Deck

The structure of the deck and its framing are crucial to the soundness of a Friendship's hull. Moreover, the decking must be tightly joined to keep the vessel dry below. Therefore, *Dictator*'s owner took special care to fortify her decking.

Dictator's deck beams had originally been 3-by-3-inch solid oak timber; where curved beams were needed, as in the three curved members that bridged the three-foot space between cabin and cockpit, the original builder had simply sawed the beams to shape. But curve-sawed timbers are much weaker than timbers in which the camber is either natural to the shape of the wood, or built in by artificial means. *Dictator*'s restorer used a modern method for putting in the curve: he fashioned four-ply laminated timber of 1-by-3⅜-inch fir strips, which he bent over a pattern while their adhesive set.

The new owner also selected ultrasturdy materials for the cabin. He built up the top with three layers of ¼-inch plywood, creating a far stronger structure than was possible with standard ¾-inch stock. All three layers were glued together and then cinched down tight with 400 screws.

This view into Dictator's undecked cabin reveals the careful joinery that gives her hull the solidity—and the beauty—of fine cabinet work. The ceiling of 1¾-by-⅜-inch cypress strips is now complete. A temporary sole has been installed. To protect it from rot, and to bring out the grain of the wood, the owner varnished each piece three times before fitting it on, and gave a fourth coat of varnish to the completed assembly. Topsides, the deck planks have been screwed in place, the screw holes bunged and the deck sanded. The coaming and cabin sides have been bent to shape, fastened to the deck beams, primed with white lead paint, ready to receive the cabin top.

Enduring Friendship

There is a saying among down-East boatmen that of most old Friendship sloops all that remains is "a pair of trailboards, a pile of rot, and a damned good pump." The collection of parts at right, salvaged from *Dictator* by Newman, is a case in point. The trailboards were carved by the wife of the builder, Robert McLain; their design, an arabesque of red cherries, was his trademark. The life ring dates from the Chesney era, the 40-odd years between 1925 and 1971. The bronze-rimmed porthole was put in by the builder. So was the weathered remnant of the original deck beam, which is carved with *Dictator*'s official document numbers, issued in 1904 and registered with the U.S. Coast Guard for the life of the boat. The pump, of indeterminate age, was located in *Dictator*'s cockpit, where the skipper could pump her out whenever he could spare a moment.

Dictator's immaculately refurbished cabin includes a pair of V-berths in the forecastle, and a settee bunk in the main cabin opposite the top-loading icebox and stove. In addition two quarter berths fit aft of the companionway, and the sloop's head is tucked in the forecastle under the brown cushion. Book racks, shelves and 12 drawers provide storage for galley utensils and tools, plus gear for five passengers.

The one small remnant of Dictator's original wood construction is this rectangular piece of the 1904 keel, dovetailed for sentiment's sake into a shallow notch cut into the new keel. The owner has identified both the new keel and the insert with a carved date.

A Personal Touch Below

One aspect in which the restored *Dictator* departed radically from the original is the furnishings of its cabin. Gone are the fish wells, bait boxes and net lockers. In their place, the owner has installed a full range of family cruising amenities, each of them a superb example of custom workmanship and convenience. There are hand-carved dish racks and fiddle rails, and handsome plaid cushion covers for the five bunks. The countertop is hard-wearing white Formica, trimmed with teak. *Dictator's* new cabin sole is made of showy, dark teak and light-toned holly. A wood-burning stove is neatly tucked under the galley countertop.

The dovetailed joints and thumb pull on this drawer are typical of the fine cabinetry belowdecks. These details, plus the hand-turned fiddle rail on the shelf above it and the wood trim on the bulkhead behind, were the work of a professional cabinetmaker.

A cast-iron, wood-burning stove rests in a stainless-steel-lined niche tailored to its dimensions. In cold weather it serves as both cookstove and cabin heater; during warm spells the owner covers it with the detachable Formica lid shown here, and substitutes a portable alcohol unit for the wood-burner.

Rigging Out

Finishing up three years of restoration work, *Dictator*'s owner spent two hard days setting up the rigging and bending on the sail. He had two guidelines to follow in planning the rig: the height of the old but still serviceable fir mast, a legacy of the previous owners, and the traditional methods and materials used for the original Friendships. But wherever he could, he substituted sturdier types of line, wire or hardware, as in the special-order bridles, stays, blocks and fittings shown here.

Dictator's sails, the first season, were a suit of cotton sails salvaged from another Friendship, the burned-out 37-foot *Emmie B.* out of Boothbay. But *Dictator* was six feet shorter than the *Emmie B.*, so the sails were a bit baggy. The newly launched sloop sailed well, however, so the owner used the old sails to draw up measurements, slightly reduced to fit, for the fine new Dacron suit he ordered the next year.

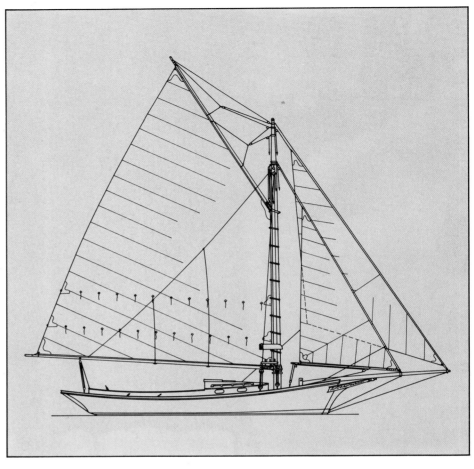

The restored Dictator's sail plan hews closely to tradition: a gaff-rigged mainsail, a club-footed staysail, and a loose-footed jib on the forestay. One minor departure: reef points on the mainsail were reduced from the conventional three rows to two.

Dictator's new bowsprit (below, left) meets traditional Friendship sloop specifications: her 10-foot overhang is nearly one third her overall length. Trailboards are carved, gilded elaborations of McLain's originals (page 93). The jib's roller reefing is a modern addition, as are the gooseneck bands (below, right) that hold the new boom to the mast and support a row of sturdy belaying pins.

Dictator's halyards, stays, lazy jacks and shrouds converge atop her mast (below). Together they support 761 square feet of sail. Oak gaff jaws are a replacement for a bronze and leather saddle. The blocks that handle the running rigging (right) have wooden shells of iron-hard lignum vitae and sheaves and beckets of bronze.

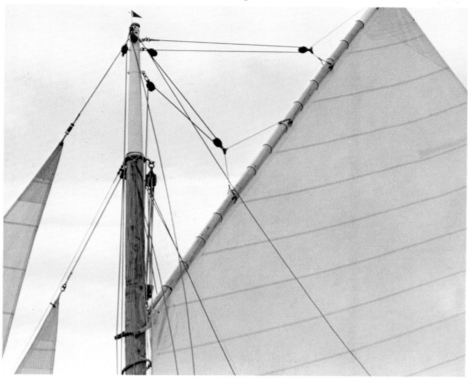

Except for lignum vitae deadeyes, standing rigging is modern: synthetic lanyards for tarred hemp between the deadeyes; stainless-steel stays for those of iron; bronze straps for iron in the chain plates. At right is a close-up of a deadeye with a lanyard rove through it. On old vessels with hemp shrouds, the deadeye lanyards were cinched up as the shrouds stretched; Newman sets his once a season.

Reaping the Rewards

The fully restored Dictator displays an elegance beyond that of even the proudest working boats among the original Friendship sloops. The white paint on the deckhouse, cockpit coaming, toe rails, bowsprit and on the spars is a traditional feature of early Friendships; but the fir and teak brightwork, the bronze deck hardware, and the handsomely nibbed and painted king plank are all touches that distinguish Dictator as the special pride of a serious cruising man.

With owner Jarvis Newman at the wheel, a brisk southwesterly sends Dictator surging across Mount Western Way. Newman calls his restored craft "a steady, sturdy delight," and says she is easy to manage singlehanded, even without reefing, in winds up to 30 knots. An unusually strong sailer to windward for a gaff-rigged boat, she has proved herself a repeated winner against other vintage sloops in seasonal regattas held by Maine's Friendship Sloop Society.

4 Restoring a classic powerboat to mint condition can sometimes be a simple and inexpensive job. In America's lake regions, where fresh waters are relatively kind to a vessel's hardware, and where many boats have always been put into dry storage at the end of each vacation season, powerboat collectors sometimes find vintage speedboats in such good shape that they require little more than, say, a new windshield and an engine tune-up to get them going. More often, however, old wooden runabouts and launches have been parked outdoors for years in back lots and odd corners of boatyards, neglected and exposed to all kinds of weather. Craft such as the boats pictured at left re-

REVIVING VINTAGE MOTORBOATS

quire extensive overhauling in order to make them seaworthy and handsome again. Frequently, a classic powerboat must have its bottom replanked, its cracked ribs replaced and a complete engine overhaul before it will be able to take the pounding of the waves while underway at speed.

To meet the growing demand for expert restoration of vintage powerboats, more than a score of small professional shipyards now specialize in rebuilding old wooden runabouts from the keel up. Typical is the Vintage Boat and Motorcar Company, in Holderness, New Hampshire. There three full-time craftsmen do all the engine, carpentry and refinishing work, including the bleaching, staining and sanding of the hulls, decks and brightwork, and the brushing on of up to six coats of marine varnish. When they have completed their work, they bring in outside experts for such specialty jobs as replacing antique upholstery and rechroming old fittings. On any given day, Vintage may be working on three or four separate boats in different stages of restoration—as is the case in the photographs on the following pages.

The complete restoration job for an 18- to 25-foot wooden speedboat takes approximately four to six weeks and can cost up to $7,500, depending on the original condition of the boat and the authenticity of its reconstruction. The restoration costs increase dramatically for larger boats. One Connecticut advertising executive spent $150,000 to restore a 38-foot Elco cruiser to perfect condition, down to the last copper fastening—a chore that took 22,000 man-hours spread over three years.

Included in these labors is the sometimes Herculean task of bringing a vintage engine back to life. At a minimum, these motors must be hauled out of the boat and steam cleaned. Then they are disassembled piece by piece. Worn-out valves, gear assemblies and other parts often must be replaced with good ones before the engine can be rebuilt. And since many of the manufacturers of old marine power plants have been out of business for years, parts must be scrounged up from old machine shops, cannibalized from a second engine of the same model—or fabricated from scratch.

Despite the need for time and money, thousands of powerboaters proudly own classic boats, and the yearly amount of restoration work is on the rise. Owners of popular old craft like the Elcos, Chris-Crafts and Gar Woods have organized clubs that hold annual regattas. At these gala affairs, the fully restored boats are entered both in speed races and in various *concourses d'élégances,* in which they are judged for the quality and the authenticity of their restoration. Besides the excitement of such competition, these refurbished classics, if properly maintained, provide owners with many seasons of delightful boating. Their elegant hulls slip through the water with little drag, while their padded cockpits and low-vibration vintage engines make them excellent riding craft by today's standards of performance. As the owner of a restored 26-foot Chris-Craft from the 1920s said after cruising along at 25 mph, "It's just like sitting in a rocking chair."

In the back lot of a New England marina two carpenters and a prospective buyer estimate the amount of work that will have to go into the restoration of a 50-year-old speedboat.

Down to the Bare Bones

After a generation of use—followed by decades of neglect—even the soundest old wooden hulls weaken and rot. Thus, the first step in the restoration of any classic powerboat is to make the craft structurally sound. Wherever rot has barely begun, wooden ribs and other structural members can be treated with a chemical restorative called "Git"-Rot, which temporarily arrests the decay and prevents further deterioration. But most often the skeleton and skin are so far gone that the only remedy is major surgery—replacing the craft's disintegrating anatomy with duplicate pieces made from fresh wood.

The carpentry performed on the powerboat at right and on the following two pages is typical of the work required to restore a classic powerboat to mint condition. The boat, a 22-foot mahogany racer, was originally built in Detroit in 1925, then raced in Tampa, Florida, before being retired to an old barn in New England. Rescued by a local powerboat buff, the old hulk was brought to a boatyard that specializes in restorations. More than 75 per cent of the original structural wood had to be replaced before the boat could venture onto the water once again.

In the main workroom of a restoration shop called the Vintage Boat and Motorcar Company, a carpenter begins to remove the rotted planks from a 50-year-old powerboat as the first step in its restoration. Over the next six months a team of craftsmen, using original materials wherever possible, will recondition and refinish the boat's hull, rebuild its engine, reupholster its cockpit and rechrome its fittings and hardware.

A carpenter begins to strip the bottom planking from an upturned powerboat by clipping off the copper rivets that were used to bind the planks to the ribs. The so-called chine plank has already been freed from the rivets and lies intact on the floor. With the chine plank off, a rotted layer of canvas waterproofing material and the diagonally laid interior planking can be removed.

Before taking off the second outside plank a workman loosens its rib-fastening screws near the bow. To find the screw positions, he uses a piece of sandpaper to clear the bottom paint away from the portions of the plank directly over the interior ribs. Then he uses a hole saw to cut away the wood around the rivets. All the outside planks are numbered and saved by the carpenters. Later they will be used as templates for cutting new planks from fresh mahogany boards.

At the stern of the boat, where the rot is most severe, a carpenter carefully works to free a disintegrating piece of the original mahogany transom frame from the bottom planking and the rabbeted chine log in the corner of the hull. Before undertaking this delicate task of removing bad ribs, he must extract the builder's screws and odd tacks and nails used over the years to patch the boat.

With the old rib clamped as a template onto a fresh piece of lumber, the carpenter measures its width to re-create its pattern. After completing the outline, he will cut out the new piece on an electric band saw, then shape and fit it with files and chisels until it matches the original piece. This will be repeated until every rotted piece of wood on the boat has been replaced with a duplicate.

Duplicated pieces of the stern section are fitted together and then put in their appropriate position on the boat. Afterward, these pieces will be treated with a wood preservative and screwed down permanently. As a final step, new mahogany transom planks will be installed in order to make the antique boat watertight once again.

When all the paint has been removed, a special bleaching solution is brushed on the planks' surface. This bleaches out old oil and weathering stains ingrained in the wood. After applying the bleach, MacDonald leaves the wood to dry overnight. On the following day, the planks will look pale and monochromatic, but the natural grains in the boards reappear with the first coat of finish.

Master craftsman Alan MacDonald, who supervises all the refinishing tasks at Vintage Boat and Motorcar Company, begins work on the topsides of a 1925 Hackercraft by scraping away layers of old finish that have been treated with a paint-removing solvent, similar to ordinary household paint remover. A second application of the paste will take off the blue undercoating paint.

MacDonald and a helper sand the bleached planks with a fine grade of silicon carbide sandpaper as the final step prior to staining and varnishing. Both men sand with the grain of the boards to avoid whorl marks that would show through the final finish.

Layers of Perfection

When refinishing the topsides and deck of vintage boats, like the two craft shown here and overleaf, the best craftsmen apply stain, a coat of sealer and six or more coats of varnish, each laid on with loving care. But before the first brush stroke, every square inch of the old wood must be cleansed of blemishes and meticulously sanded until it is satin smooth. Then the craftsman brushes on the finish coats in as bland an environment as possible.

Varnishing should never be done in the presence of moisture or direct sunlight, both of which can hinder the curing of the varnish. The boat should be thoroughly vacuumed to be dust free, and doors and windows to the work area should be shut. One perfectionist does all his varnishing just before dawn—the time of day when the least dust is in the air. Another waits for a fresh snowfall before touching brush to wood. And a third, a real varnisher's varnisher, rhapsodizes about the possibility of varnishing a boat in the middle of the North Pacific Ocean, where the air is said to be the cleanest in the world.

Before applying the third of six coats of varnish to the deck of an 18-foot mahogany Chris-Craft, MacDonald wipes the sanded surface of the deck with a tack rag. The sticky rag—a small piece of cotton cloth that has been sprinkled with water, a few drops of turpentine and varnish, and then wrung nearly dry—picks up minute particles of dust that cling to the surface of the wood.

MacDonald brushes a coat of varnish onto the transom of the Chris-Craft. After applying a generous amount to his brush, he strokes lightly back and forth with the tip of the brush to avoid runs and to get rid of as many air bubbles as possible. When the coat has completely dried, it will be sanded so that the next coat will adhere evenly.

As the restoration of the 18-foot Chris-Craft nears completion, MacDonald and his helper reinstall the toeboards and seat mounts to wrap up the carpentry work on the cockpit. They have also stripped a coating of enamel paint off the steering wheel in order to expose the underlying flat black finish of the original bakelite material.

Before the seats are installed the workmen set the original side panels into the cockpit. Fastened by screws to the ribs of the craft, the ½-inch-thick mahogany boards have been sanded and varnished before being put into position. A final coat of varnish will be applied to the interior woodwork once all the boards are screwed down tightly.

A final restorative touch to the woodwork is the application of a stripe of polysulfide caulking compound to the narrow cracks between the mahogany deck planks. Here MacDonald squeezes some of the compound between the narrow slats of an old hatch cover. He will then work the polysulfide into the cracks with a fingertip. The strips of masking tape already laid down on the varnished surface of the planks prevent any accidental marring of the high-gloss finish.

Refurbishing the Seats

Speedboat cockpits of the '20s and '30s were richly padded in horsehair and leather, both for good looks and as protection against the pounding and vibration of high-speed travel. The two-day restoration being performed on the cockpit of the runabout pictured typifies the upholstery work involved in putting such a craft into mint condition. From their wooden backrests to the old-fashioned spring cushions, the cockpit seats are disassembled, examined for rot and wear, and rebuilt or, where necessary, replaced.

On this particular boat the bulk of the original horsehair cushion stuffing was salvageable, but the 50-year-old seat covers had so deteriorated that the upholsterer ended up sewing a whole new set from Naugahyde chosen to match the color and grain of the original leather.

An upholstery specialist uses a claw hammer to strip off the assorted nails and tacks embedded in the deteriorated backrest of a vintage speedboat's cockpit (right). After replacing one of the rotted plywood backrest pieces, he lays strips of cotton padding over the interior wooden braces (below, left), and then tacks down a swath of horsehair stuffing from the original backrest (below, right).

To fabricate a cover in classic style for the backrest of the driver's seat, the craftsman affixes strips of decorative welting to the two separate pieces of red Naugahyde upholstery material. The welting, made by folding a 1-inch strip of black vinyl around a length of ¼-inch-diameter nylon cord, covers the seam between the two larger pieces of upholstery and also helps keep the seat cover waterproof.

The completed seat cover is attached to the wooden backrest (above) with a staple gun. Afterward the craftsman returns the finished cushion to the speedboat's cockpit (left), where it fits in snugly between the sides of the craft, as did the original version when the boat was first built in the 1930s.

A workman at a chrome-plating shop plunges an assortment of early powerboat fittings into a caustic wash (above) that removes all traces of the old, corroded chrome and nickel. When the fittings have been thoroughly cleansed, the workman dries off each one with a jet of compressed air (right).

A New Silver Gleam

Probably the most specialized job in the restoration of a vintage boat is the refinishing of its original nickel- or chrome-plated hardware. Portholes, deck cleats and ventilator cowls—often badly corroded and invariably tarnished—must be removed, catalogued and sent to an electroplating shop, like the one pictured here in Newburyport, Massachusetts.

At the shop each piece of hardware is cleaned and buffed. Then it is wired into an electrical terminal, and dipped into an electrolytic solution of sulfuric acid and dissolved metal. When current is sent from the terminal, the dissolved metal adheres to the piece. Each fitting must be plated with an undercoat of copper followed by a layer of nickel. Then most powerboat restorers add a finishing layer of chromium—giving the piece a hard, gleaming surface that holds up well in both fresh and salt water.

Some purists—especially those with craft dating back to the 1920s before the process of chrome-plating was widely available—omit the chrome and finish off with nickel. Nickel-plated fittings have a rich, warm gloss typical of the earliest powerboat hardware. But nickel is more vulnerable to the elements than is chrome, and requires frequent polishing in order to keep it in top condition.

In the final step before plating, a metalworker polishes a brass porthole on a rotary buffer to ensure that the layer of chrome will adhere evenly.

*A master mechanic begins to dismantle a 12-cylinder Liberty engine
by unbolting the camshaft housing from a row of cylinder heads.
Then he will be able to remove the cylinders—each cast separately
from a nickel-alloy metal and bolted onto the aluminum engine block
—in order to work on the pistons. The monstrous engine, popular
with boat racers in the '20s and '30s, was originally built for use in
World War I aircraft and could generate more than 500 horsepower.
When fully restored this engine will power a 33-foot 1931 Gar Wood-
designed powerboat at a top speed of over 50 miles per hour.*

Resuscitating an Engine

To get an old marine engine going again after years of idleness, a mechanic like the expert working on the inboard power plant pictured here must have the skills and patience of a sorcerer. To begin with, the engine and transmission must be taken out of the boat, and any external buildup of rust and corrosion blasted off with live steam. After this process both of these components are completely taken apart. Old pistons, rings and valves are carefully extracted from the engine block, and then cleaned and examined for wear. Frequently these parts are so worn out or corroded that new ones have to be fabricated from scratch—the original manufacturers having gone out of business decades ago. Moreover, all of the newly made parts must be machined to tolerances of a few ten-thousandths of an inch in order for them to mesh properly in the engine.

Finally, the engine's entire electrical system must be retimed, often without the aid of the manufacturer's manual. Coaxing an engine like the 1917 Liberty model at left back into working order will require more than $5,000 in parts and labor. But, as one dedicated workman observed, "When you hear the way this baby runs, you'll know it was worth it."

With the engine partly disassembled, the cylinders are checked for scratches and grooves in their walls. To restore a worn cylinder the mechanic will use a fine silicon carbide reamer that can scrape out carbon deposits and microscopic nicks. Later he will attach a newly machined set of steel rings to the five-inch-diameter pistons to allow the engine to reach full compression.

The tip of a screwdriver, used to chip away the crust of a broken surface weld, exposes an ancient crack in one of the engine's 12 cylinders. The damaged cylinder will be rewelded in a temperature-controlled oven in order to prevent heat distortion.

In an open lot behind the restoration shop, a steam-cleaning apparatus removes years of grease and grime from the transmission of another old marine engine. The jet of steam roars into the nooks and crannies of the transmission housing, exposing any cracks or defects found in the old cast metal.

Ready for Launching

After the long weeks of being dismantled, reframed, replanked, reupholstered and even repowered, a boat like the 26-foot Chris-Craft shown here goes into the final stages of assembly before taking to the water. The boatworks team installs the rebuilt engine, connects the instruments on the dashboard to their terminals, and hooks up the gas lines, the battery and the internal wiring. Then they apply a last coat of varnish, and when it has dried they screw down all the rechromed fittings. Finally, they take up buffing rags to make a last gratifying pass over the boat to bring its brightwork to a high polish.

For this Chris-Craft, the whole process took six weeks and cost $7,500—a good piece of change for any boatowner. But the result adds up to a boat that, according to one of the restorers, "is as good or better than it was when it was new." On its reconditioned Kermath engine, shown at right, the sporty speedboat can cruise at 25 mph and can wind up in short bursts to 40 mph, as it did for its first owners more than 50 years ago.

A lovingly restored six-cylinder Kermath engine lies snugly in its compartment moments after installation. A popular marine power plant throughout the '20s and '30s, this Kermath can generate 225 horsepower from the cylinders positioned beneath its distinctive camshaft cover. The brass box rigged on the portside is a restored Holley downdraft carburetor—a patented device with a gas shutoff valve to prevent the engine from running without adequate oil pressure.

A chrome-plated gas cap, equipped with a spring-loaded latch that makes a watertight seal when it is fastened, gleams on the striped deck planking at the runabout's stern.

The Chris-Craft's mahogany hull gets one final dash of spit and polish outside the restoration shop before being shipped to its owner. The bright strips of polysulfide deck caulking and chrome on the seven-foot-long bow accentuate the long, lean lines of this classic runabout.

FINE TOUCHES ON CLASSIC CRAFT

This solid-brass spotlight, offered by catalogue to powerboatmen in 1924, displays the elegant craftsmanship once typical even of factory-produced accessories. By adjusting a reflecting mirror behind the light bulb, it can be made to function either as a narrow focus spot or as a wide-angle flood.

During the vintage boatbuilding business years before World War II, when every private vessel was at least partially custom-made, a special kind of loving care was lavished on their fittings. If a boat designer or builder was not able to find just the right brass binnacle or bronze cleat at the ship chandler's, he would get his local machine shop to make one.

Thus a small boatyard such as Fay & Bowen, producers of fine custom power launches at Geneva, New York, would order up a gracefully curved brass grab rail like the one on page 122. Designers such as John Alden or L. Francis Herreshoff would turn out even such workaday items as tillers and cleats in their own workshops, to their own exacting specifications. Nameboards were carved and ornamented by hand, belaying pins and bow chocks and blocks were individually whittled or cast into shape. Even the purveyors of the first assembly-line boats, such as Elco or Chris-Craft, would strive for a certain custom look in the fittings of their family runabouts, launches and cruisers.

Today restorers of classic boats and builders of classic reproductions still go to great lengths to finish off their craft with the same befitting elegance. They spend their spare hours prospecting junk yards, canvassing antique shops, perusing marine archives and searching out oldtime craftsmen to uncover just the right fastening, bell or deadeye. "The only place I know to get a proper oak mast hoop is from one small shop in Newbury, Massachusetts," said Bob Kelly, owner of a gaff-rigged ketch on pages 126-127. But the search for authenticity is invariably worth it. Besides the satisfaction of owning an object that is old and handsomely salty, any skipper who suits his fittings to the style and period of his boat knows that they will not only look best, but will generally work best as well.

The helmsman's post pictured here of this 1926 Elco features a brass-trimmed wheel and a brass binnacle flanked by a pair of lamps.

Small Craft Adornings

Deeply carved lettering and scrollwork, highlighted with gold leaf, enrich the helmsman's backrest on this 1970 reproduction of a fancy rowing boat of the turn of the century. The knotted lines on either side are part of an old-fashioned steering device known as a yoke. The helmsman, seated in the stern, held a line in each hand, pulling on the appropriate one to turn the yoke, visible behind the ensign staff.

A demountable brass oarlock rides in a scalloped socket, which in turn is screwed to the sheer clamp inside the gunwale of a small wooden skiff. The rope bumper tacked in the groove of the skiff's rub rail is a handsome —and highly practical—device for fending off other craft in minor collisions.

An adjustable foot brace, called a stretcher, located aft of the rowing thwart and adjustable to the length of an oarsman's legs, was a standard device on pulling boats. Though strength was the primary requirement for such braces, many were decorated —carved or lathe-turned, then varnished or shellacked to bring out the natural grain.

Elegant in its simplicity, the bow of this Maine dory displays traditional painted planking, varnished rail and a painter rove through hawseholes.

The launch Aida II was turned out in 1907 by Fay & Bowen to operate on the fashionable Finger Lakes in upstate New York. Her modern owners have restored her turn-of-the-century opulence with a cockpit of gleaming brass and soft-sheened leather. The motor, which is located forward of the wicker chairs, is a 1912 crank-start engine.

Curlicue brass grab rails, a flourish frequently used by Fay & Bowen on their pleasure craft, were salvaged from a sister ship of Aida II. The protective brass along the cutwater is among the original fittings on the launch.

Posh Powerboat Accessories

Appointed in the manner of a first-class sports roadster, this antique Chris-Craft has glove-leather upholstered seat cushions, wool-tartan lap robes, and an oak-framed convertible top that folds down in fair weather and raises in foul to enclose the entire forward passenger area. Most of these details were already on the boat when she was launched as a production model in 1929.

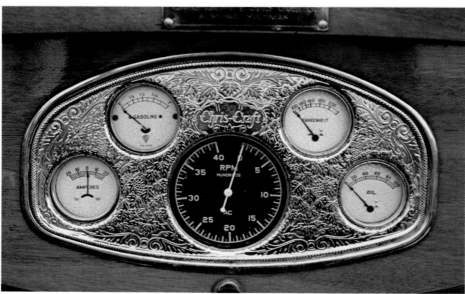

This instrument panel with ornamental chasing engraved on a chrome-plated frame also belonged to a sister ship. Since the original chrome was worn thin from years of exposure, the panel has been replated, and a missing dial face for the large central speed gauge has been replaced by a part from another instrument panel. The deeply toned dashboard is made of solid mahogany planking, varnished to a high gloss.

Snug Appointments

Showpiece in the elegant cabin of the 40-foot cruiser Turtle, built in 1931, is a wood-burning stove replica with brass frame and soapstone face. The butternut bulkheads and drop-leaf table were built into the original boat. The dinner plates are white ironstone fetched from England. Only the goblets are modern—a concession to practicality in nonbreakable geranium-colored plastic.

A fold-up chrome-plated sink gleams from a bulkhead aboard the 1928 ketch Viking. Elegant and compact, this vintage unit is boxed in a four-inch-deep mahogany cabinet that folds down (right) to reveal a handsome, functional wash basin, pump and soap dish.

A kerosene lantern hangs on gimbals in Viking's main cabin. The smoke bell above its chimney catches both heat and carbon. The unit is as old as the boat itself, but ships' chandlers continue to carry almost identical models of this prized and practical fixture.

Stored away in a safe spot when it is not arranged on the table at mealtime, the ironstone dinnerware aboard the Turtle stands with polished pewter behind the leaded windows of a butternut cabinet that matches exactly the cruiser's original butternut paneling.

Handsome Topside Fittings

A heavy brass fog bell, affixed to the square-sided, glassed-in cabin of the antique power cruiser Phoenix, carries a bell rope knotted with crown sennits and Turk's heads. Like the boat—a 1928 Elco—the fog bell is a genuine antique; but as with the lamp pictured on the previous page, excellent replicas can be purchased today.

A stout metal cruciform bitt, one of a pair on Phoenix's quarter-deck, belays a stern docking line. Ten inches high and cast of heavy marine brass, the bitt is a rare custom version of the workman-like wooden bollards often used to secure the anchor rode on vintage wood boats.

Sturdy spars and fittings of the Viking exemplify the functional beauty
in the details of a classic gaff rig. Hoops of varnished oak, bent
around the mizzen and closed with copper rivets, are lashed to the
luff of the sail to hold it to the mast. Lines called lizard strings run
between the hoops to keep them aligned when the sail is hoisted.
Wooden bearings—or parrels—of hard-wearing lignum vitae guide
the mizzen gaff jaws. The painted iron strap for the gooseneck holds
two iron belaying pins. Similar straps at the end of the main boom
hold the main sheet purchase—twin blocks with outer shells of ash,
an extremely tough wood that takes on a rich gloss under varnish.

5 When a modern boatman makes his maiden voyage on a classic craft, he is likely to find himself handling a strange assortment of lines and facing a multitude of fittings, spars and other seamanly apparatus that he has never encountered before. Aboard a schooner like the cruising vessel at left, for example, he will have to hank on the jib while balanced on a bowsprit. When he raises the mainsail and foresail, he will be wrestling with two lines for each sail —a throat halyard and a peak halyard—instead of the single halyard to be found on a modern, jib-headed rig. As he hauls on the halyards, whether aboard a schooner or some other classic vessel, he must know the proper

OF RIGS AND SEAMANSHIP

height to raise the peak to give the sail its proper draft *(pages 142-143)*. And in certain wind conditions, he will be setting archaic pieces of canvas called topsails, shown on pages 152-153.

These and other tasks of seamanship aboard a classic boat may appear puzzling at first; but they are relatively easy to learn. And once the boatman has the knack of them, he will find the rig of a classic craft to be a masterpiece of simplicity—and function. For every one of these rigs was designed to go out in any weather, to bring home the fish, or the lobster or clams, or whatever cargo provided the livelihood of the boat's owner. A halyard that jammed, or a spar that broke, was cash out of the family pocket, both in terms of a day's work lost and of cost in time and money for replacement. Thus the rigging was not only built to be as stout and simple as possible, but was fashioned out of easily obtainable—and easily workable—materials: local wood for spars, inexpensive three-strand manila for lines, wood hoops with marline or hemp lashings to hold the luff of the sail to the mast.

On most of the smaller craft, such as the sprit-rigged dories, wherries and other boats on pages 130-137, there was no standing rigging whatever. Sheets were single part lines running straight inboard from the foot or the clew; halyards, if they existed at all, were also single part lines led through a hole drilled in the mast. Most of the masts were unstayed, designed to be lifted out at day's end—or when the boat reached a handy anchorage or a fishing ground. These unstayed masts often were made to rotate so that when, say, a lobsterman reached his potline, he could simply let go of the sheet and allow the sail to swing harmlessly forward with the wind, rather than being forced to haul in the sail and hold head to wind, while trying simultaneously to take aboard lobster traps.

The business of shortening sail in heavy weather also was simpler—if a bit less elegant—aboard some of these older craft than on most of today's more mechanized racing or cruising boats. A small sprit-rigged boat could remove the sprit and fold its quadrilateral sail into a triangle; and it often had brailing lines that served as jiffy-reefing devices with little more than a tug on the line *(page 134)*. A few small craft were equipped with multiple mast steps so that the sailor could add or remove a mast and thus alter sail area according to weather conditions *(page 135)*.

Even the schooner, which is considered by the majority of modern boatmen to be a sailor's gymnasium because of its cat's cradle of stays and running gear, is, in the hands of a well-initiated crew, a wonderfully convenient and efficient rig. For shortening, adding and balancing sail according to the weight of wind and point of sail at any given moment, a schooner is the most flexible of boats. As shown on page 155, on a bright, boisterous afternoon a medium-sized schooner reaching for home can pile on a half dozen sails. But when the weather turns sour and all hands but the helmsman are below, she can ride in a gale just off the wind under reefed-down foresail alone.

Striking the foresail, one crewman eases the throat and peak halyards and another gathers in the sails as the helmsman of this down-East schooner glides downwind into a Maine harbor.

The Sprit Rig

The most common way of carrying a sail on classic boats under about 20 feet long —dories, wherries, beach skiffs, gunning boats and the like—was the sprit rig. This is a three- or four-sided sail held out from the mast on a narrow, lightweight spar —the sprit—which is approximately the same length as the mast, and which braces the sail at a single point, either at the head or at the clew.

In the more usual form of the rig, the sprit is secured near the base of the mast, and then extends diagonally upward to the sail's upper outside corner, or peak *(right)*. This setup accommodates more sail area for a given spar length than does the second basic variation, in which the sprit is set horizontally *(far right, bottom)*. But the horizontal rig offers its own advantage; it has a lower center of effort, and therefore greater stability.

In either of its incarnations, the sprit rig is wonderfully easy to set up and to handle. As there are no shrouds or stays, a sailor can rig his boat in seconds by simply fitting the mast into its step. Once underway, he has only two lines to contend with —the sheet that trims the sail, and a line, called a snotter, that positions the sprit to shape the sail. At the end of the day he furls the sail by rolling it up around the sprit, and then lashes the sprit to the mast with the snotter. Both spars are short enough so that when the sailor unsteps the rig he can stow sail, mast and sprit right in the boat.

The basic spritsail rig for a small skiff consists of a four-sided sail held aloft by a diagonal sprit typically mounted along the sail's starboard side. The top of the sprit slips into the peak of the sail, and provides tension at the sail's head. The sprit's lower end, or heel, hitches to the mast by means of an adjustable line called a snotter. The sail's luff is laced to the mast, and the mainsheet runs directly from the clew to the helmsman's hand.

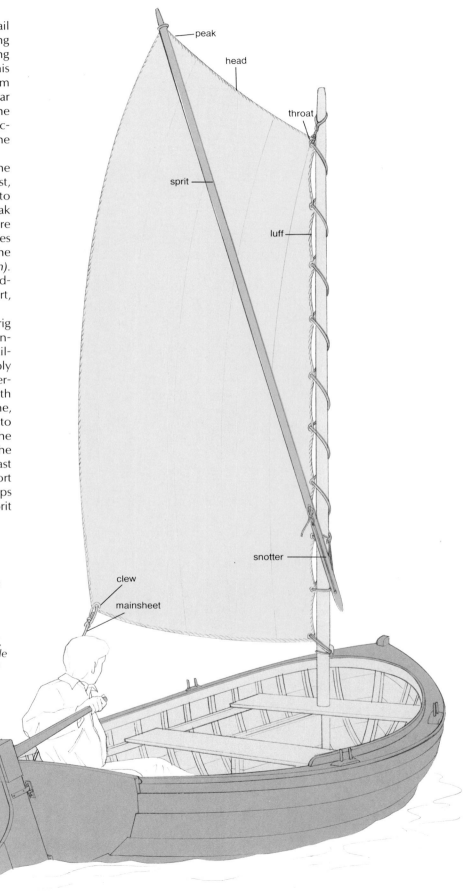

To secure the mast on most small sprit-rigged boats (directly below), the sailor runs the mast heel through a hole in the thwart to a mast block where it pivots as the boat changes tack. With this arrangement, he usually steps the mast each time he goes sailing. On many larger boats (bottom) the mast runs through the deck and remains stepped for the season. To ease turning, the mast partners are often lined with leather and the mast step faced with brass.

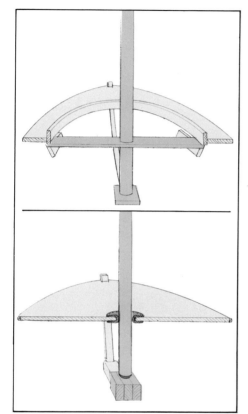

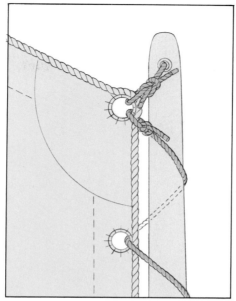

A standard method of attaching the sail to the top of a removable mast is a simple loop of line rove through the sail's throat and through a hole in the masthead, where it is tied with a square knot. The sail is then laced to the mast as shown and raised into position.

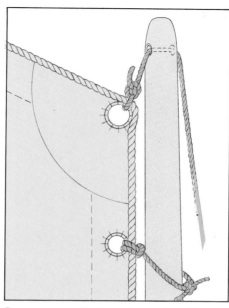

On a permanently stepped mast, the sail may be equipped with a halyard that runs through a hole in the masthead and makes fast to a cleat farther down the mast. Instead of being laced, the sail is held to the mast by robands —loops of rope tied with square knots.

On some larger classic boats like the Chesapeake Bay log canoes and sharpies, a sailor is likely to find a loose-footed triangular sail with a horizontal sprit (right). The horizontal spar is proportionately shorter —and thus easier to handle—than the more common diagonal one. This sprit is fitted into a loop at the clew of the sail and has a standard snotter rigged at the mast.

Trimming a Spritsail

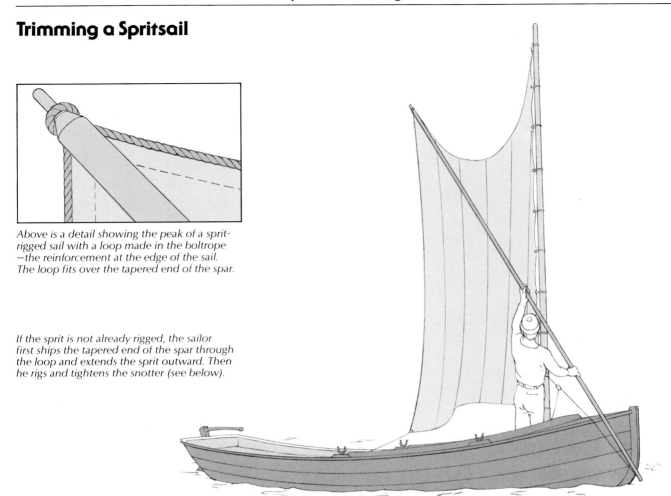

Above is a detail showing the peak of a sprit-rigged sail with a loop made in the boltrope —the reinforcement at the edge of the sail. The loop fits over the tapered end of the spar.

If the sprit is not already rigged, the sailor first ships the tapered end of the spar through the loop and extends the sprit outward. Then he rigs and tightens the snotter (see below).

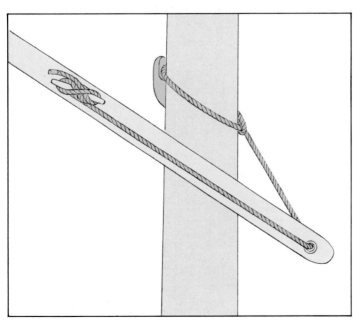

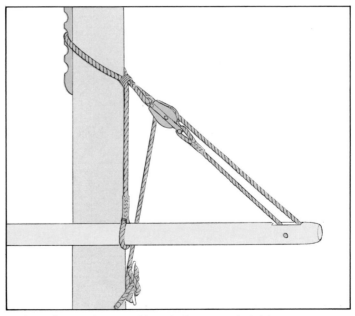

The snotter, as used on many small sprit-rigged boats, consists of a single-purchase line with a small eyesplice at one end. The snotter is looped around the mast and the working end is threaded through the eye to run down through a hole in the heel of the sprit; the line is then made fast to a cleat on the sprit. Shortening the snotter thrusts the sprit upward and aft. Loosening it allows the sprit to move forward. A thumb cleat attached to the mast holds the loop at the desired height—about one third of the way above the mast step.

On larger boats, where mechanical advantage is helpful in trimming a sprit, the snotter is often rigged with a simple tackle. The line for the tackle is spliced to a block becket and leads down through a sheave in the sprit, back up through the block, and down to a conventional cleat on the mast. A notched piece of wood affixed to the mast holds the loop of the snotter at a range of suitable heights.

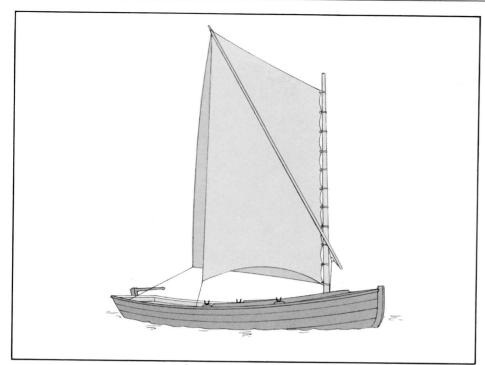

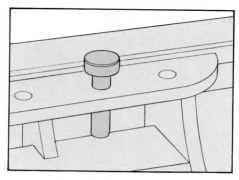

For a loose-footed spritsail to set correctly, the mainsheet must be led aft at an angle that bisects the clew of the sail (dark blue). Leading it too far forward (light blue) will produce a baggy, inefficient sail—a particular disadvantage if the helmsman is trying to sail against the wind.

Sprit-riggers often have a wooden peg at each gunwale that can be moved aft for beating, center for reaching (top), forward for running. The helmsman can take a turn around the peg and slip a hitch under the turn (bottom); the strain on the sheet will hold the line fast against the rail, and a tug will release it.

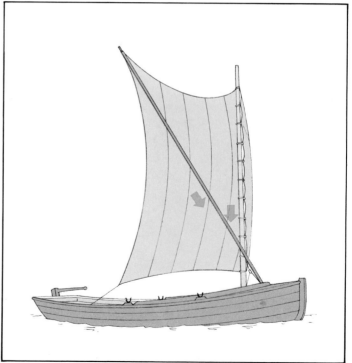

In moderate to heavy winds, a sailor can flatten his spritsail by hiking the looped end of the snotter slightly higher on the mast and tightening the snotter. This will push the peak of the sail farther out, bringing the draft forward and improving windward performance.

To add drawing power to the sail in light air, the sailor lets off the snotter and slides the loop lower on the mast: the sail then takes a fuller, curved shape. Even on boats that do not have a notched fitting to hold the snotter at different heights, friction on the cinched line tends to keep the loop wherever it is placed on the mast.

Spritsail Conversions

The fastest way to reduce sail on a sprit-rigged boat is to do what old salts call "scandalizing" the sail: the snotter is released, the sprit is slipped out of the peak and the top of the sail is allowed to flop over to leeward. The resulting sail (blue) is a triangle half as large as the original sail.

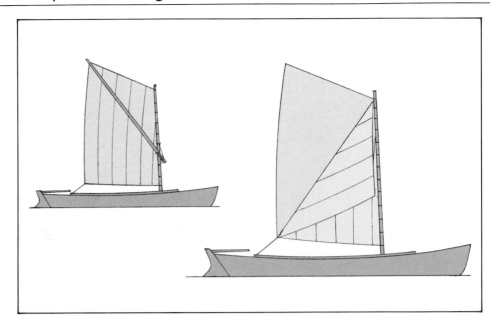

If folding the sail in half is too drastic a reduction and the sail has reef points, the helmsman can ease the halyard and snotter and take a reef in the sail, tying the reef points around the loose foot, as described on page 144. Reefing reduces sail by the amount shown in gray in the drawing far right.

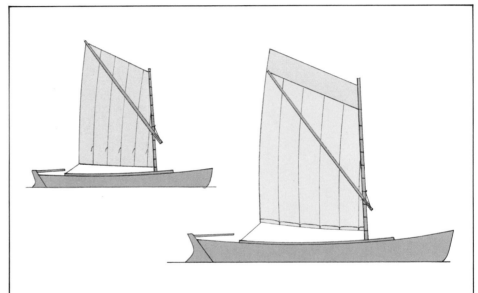

The spritsails on some sharpies have a vertical batten set in a pocket about two to three feet aft of the luff; a series of light lines called brails run horizontally from points on the batten pocket through rings on the luff, and splice into a line running down the mast. To shorten sail the skipper eases the snotter and pulls on this reefing line, bringing the batten forward to the mast and thereby reducing sail area in one easy operation by as much as a third (gray, far right). He then secures the reefing line and the snotter.

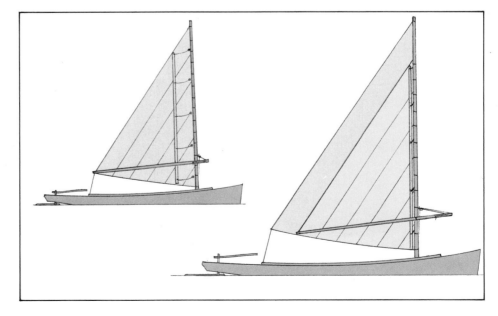

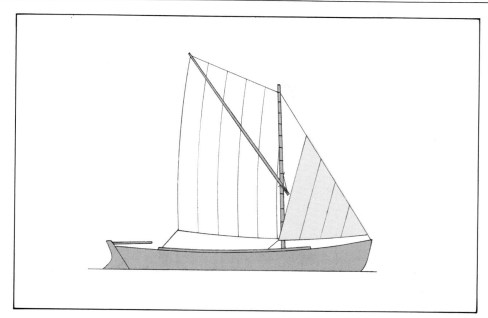

The simplest solution for adding sail in light winds is to run up a small jib. The jib can be set flying—that is, without a headstay—so the only extra gear required is a fitting to hold the tack at the stem of the boat and a block at the masthead for a jib halyard.

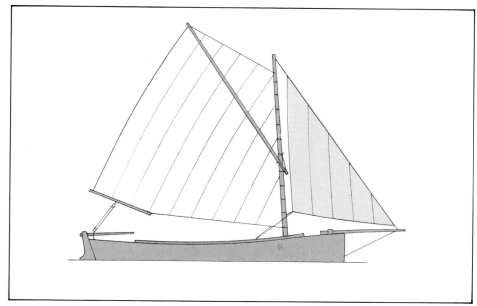

On a sprit-rigger whose mast is stepped very close to the stem, as on the Hampton boat at left, a temporary bowsprit can be fitted to the stemhead to make room for a jib. The bowsprit slides under a U-shaped fitting on the foredeck and may be rigged with a bobstay for extra support. At the leech of this mainsail is a club, a spar sometimes used on spritsails to extend sail area. The club acts as a small boom, making it possible to carry an oversized loose-footed sail that can still be trimmed properly on any point of sailing.

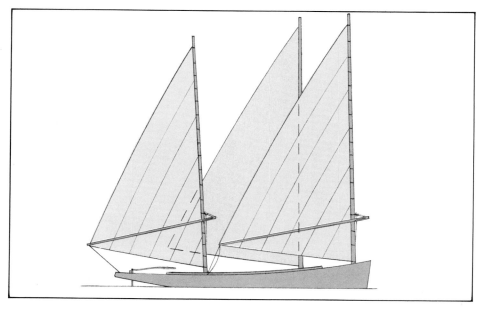

The sharpie, which carries one mast and sail (gray) in heavy winds, can carry two sails (blue) when winds lighten. To add the second sail, the helmsman moves the original mast from its step at the center to another one forward and adds a slightly smaller mast and sail to a third step farther aft.

An Eccentric Rig

Many 18th and 19th Century lifeboats and fishing boats—especially in Europe, but also in this country—carried a lugsail, a four-sided sail set from a yard extending forward of the mast. The concept of the lug remains valid: as the luff of the sail is not laced to a turbulence-producing spar, air flows over the sail in an unbroken curve, making the lug a powerful rig.

Of the many variants of the lug rig, the best driving design is the dipping-lug *(right)*, so called because each time the boat tacks, the yard and sail must be partially lowered, dipped behind the mast, and raised again on the new leeward side. This procedure is sufficiently complicated that dipping lugs were used primarily where local winds and land configurations cooperated in allowing boats to stay on a single tack for extended periods of time. If a narrow channel or an obstruction made a quick tack necessary, crews often left the sail on the wrong side, trimming it for the new angle of wind as best they could, and returning to the more favorable tack as soon as possible.

Other forms of the lug rig include the balance lug, which often carries a boom and is usually not dipped; the standing lug, which has a leading edge that tapers from throat to tack, with the tack secured at the mast; and the split lug, which has a sail divided vertically at the mast so that when the boat tacks the two parts of the sail can flop to leeward unobstructed. All lug rigs share the advantage of a relatively large spread of canvas, a low center of effort and a minimum of gear.

The dipping lugsail on this lifeboat is laced to its yard and hoisted on a halyard, which is led to the windward rail and rigged to a tackle. Hitched in this manner, the halyard acts as a shroud, helping to support the unstayed mast. The tack of the sail, forward of the mast, is also made fast on the windward rail, a few feet abaft the stem, in order to counteract the sail's tendency to sag off to leeward.

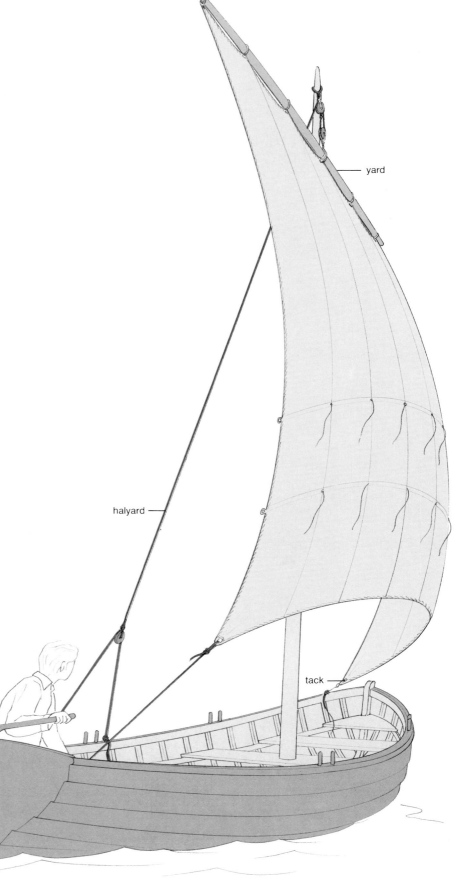

yard

halyard

tack

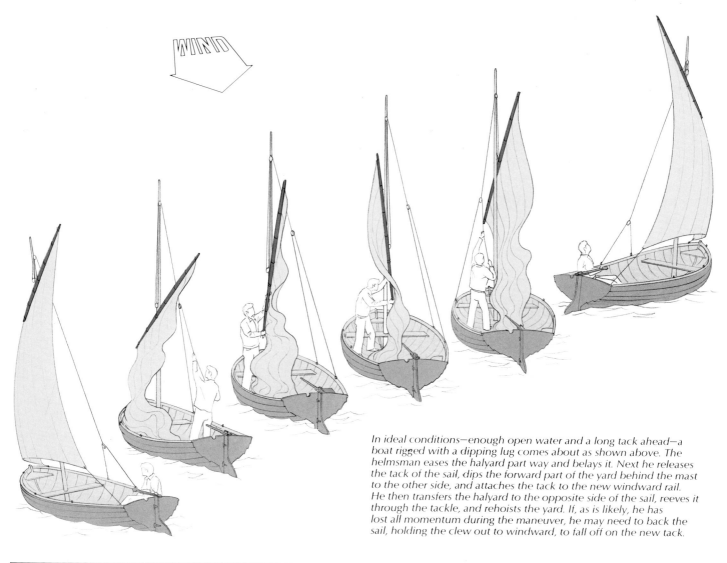

In ideal conditions—enough open water and a long tack ahead—a boat rigged with a dipping lug comes about as shown above. The helmsman eases the halyard part way and belays it. Next he releases the tack of the sail, dips the forward part of the yard behind the mast to the other side, and attaches the tack to the new windward rail. He then transfers the halyard to the opposite side of the sail, reeves it through the tackle, and rehoists the yard. If, as is likely, he has lost all momentum during the maneuver, he may need to back the sail, holding the clew out to windward, to fall off on the new tack.

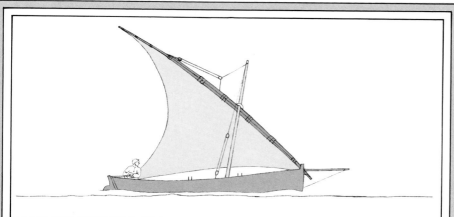

The Lateen Sail

Another rig set from a yard jutting forward of the mast—and one that has survived in the 150,000 Sunfish and Sailfish that dot the world—is the lateen. Its chief advantage is that it allows a large sail to be set from a very short mast. Devised by the Arabs and popular on the Mediterranean—its name comes from the word Latin—the lateen was brought to the United States by Italian immigrants and used on West Coast fishing boats like the felucca, above. In light air, the felucca flew a jib from the bowsprit; in heavy weather, its long flexible yard spilled excess wind from the sail, postponing the necessity of reefing.

The Basic Gaff Rig

The gaff rig uses a spar to spread the head of a four-sided, fore-and-aft sail, but unlike the sprit, which it resembles in function, the gaff is a semipermanent part of the sail. It is attached to the head of the sail by a continuous lacing and is usually raised and lowered by means of a pair of halyards—one attached to the forward end of the gaff, known as the throat, and the other to the far end, or peak.

The angle at which the gaff meets the mast varies considerably from boat to boat and depends upon the cut of the sail it supports. The length of the head is conventionally between three-fifths and two-thirds that of the foot, with the angle of the gaff varying from 30° to 40°.

The gaff was originally used primarily on larger boats where the sprit required to span the same amount of sail area would have been unmanageably long and cumbersome. By the turn of the century, however, the gaff rig had become the most common rig for workboats of all sizes —from the small catboat on these and the following four pages to the multisailed schooners on pages 150-155.

The catboat—one of the simplest of gaff-rigged craft—is a weatherly and extremely stable shoal-draft centerboarder. The boat's stout, unstayed mast, stepped exceptionally far forward, carries a single huge sail. The running rigging consists of throat and peak halyards, a mainsheet, a topping lift and a pair of lazy jacks—lines running from mast to boom on either side of the sail to prevent the folds of canvas from falling on the deck or in the water as it is lowered.

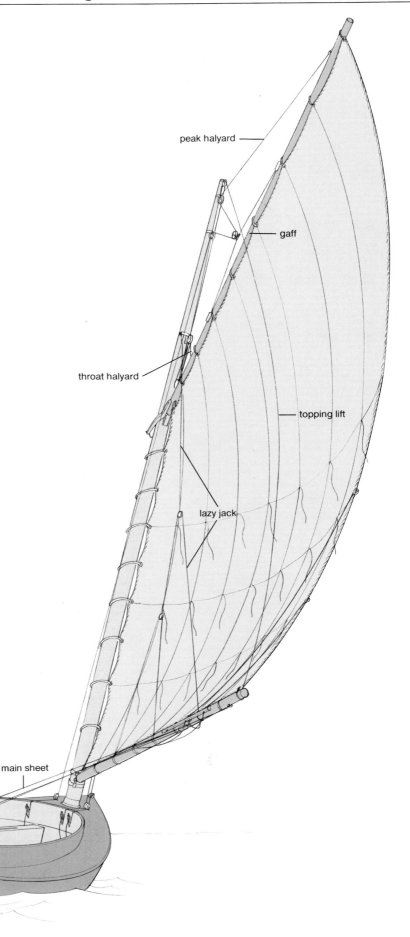

peak halyard

gaff

throat halyard

topping lift

lazy jack

main sheet

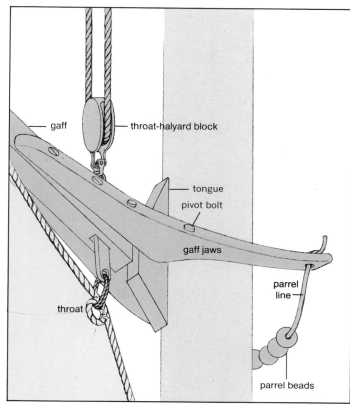

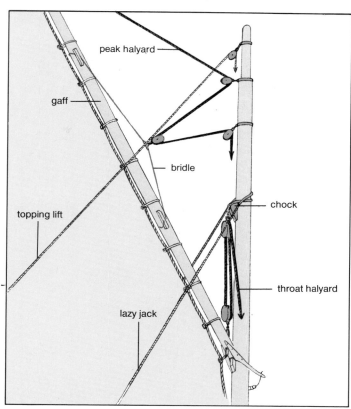

At the throat, a pair of wooden jaws fit around the mast with enough clearance to allow the gaff to move freely as the sail changes position. A so-called tongue is inserted between the jaws and the gaff proper; held with a pivot bolt, the tongue remains parallel with the mast, whatever the angle of the gaff, to distribute the gaff's thrust against the mast. A parrel line, sometimes strung with lignum vitae beads, runs through the jaw ends on the forward side of the mast. A metal fitting is bolted in a slot in the gaff; the throat halyard is shackled to its top and the throat of the sail is lashed to the bottom.

Two halyards lift the gaff. Typically, the peak halyard starts at the far end of the gaff, runs to the uppermost halyard block on the mast, and laces back to a point midway along the gaff, where it threads through another block traveling on a bridle. It then continues on to a second mast block and runs down to a turning block on the deck. The throat halyard begins at a block on the mast, runs down to a corresponding block on the gaff, returns to the mast block and down to the deck. A wood chock holds the upper throat-halyard block clear of the mast, giving the halyard a fair lead to the lower block.

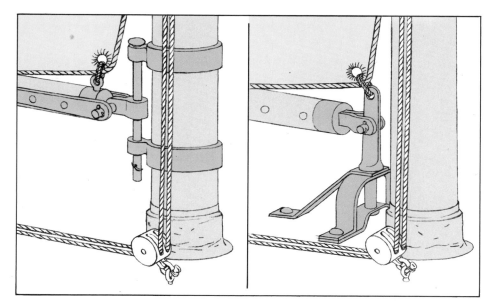

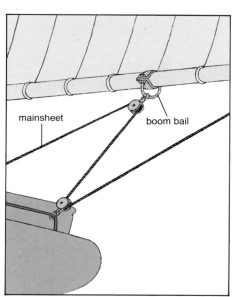

The boom—commonly clasped to the mast with jaws, as is the gaff —is often fitted with a metal gooseneck, two examples of which are shown above. In the version at left, a boom-end fitting rides up and down and swivels on a rod held by two mastbands. In the other version, a metal pedestal called a crab is fastened to the deck abaft the mast. The crab, because it is independent of the mast, reduces the strains placed on the mast by the boom.

A metal fitting called a bail helps relieve the twisting strain placed on the boom by the changing angle of the mainsheet. When the boat is close-hauled, the mainsheet block is at the bottom of the bail; when the boom swings outboard, the block slides inboard, thus equalizing the stress on the boom.

Bending On and Hoisting

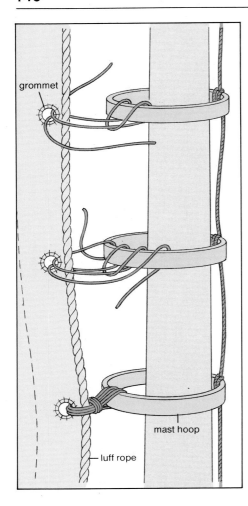

In a traditional method of bending the sail to the mast (left), wooden mast hoops are seized to grommets on the sail's luff. Using light marline, a tag hitch is taken around the hoop, and the free ends passed through the grommet (top). The ends are then passed back through the hoop (center), and several crossing turns taken around all parts (bottom). The seizing must be just slack enough so the hoops lie at right angles to the luff rope. To keep the hoops evenly spaced and help prevent jamming when the sail is raised, a light line is sometimes connected to the forward edges of the hoops.

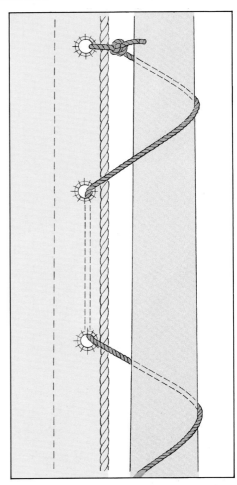

Many gaff-rig sailors prefer to lace the sail to the mast with the lacing pattern shown at right. Although hoops provide convenient footholds for climbing aloft, they cost more than lacing and may break when the gaff jaws are dropped on them too quickly. In addition, a sail laced to the mast in this fashion can be raised without risk of jamming, and the tension of its luff can be easily adjusted.

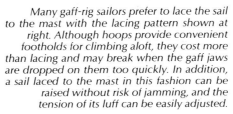

A continuous lacing of marline hitches holds the head of the sail to the gaff. The lacing begins at the throat and runs along the gaff until it reaches the peak. At the peak, several turns of line are taken around the gaff and through the peak cringle, with the middle turn going around the gaff alone. The end of the line is then rove through a hole in the end of the gaff and secured at the cringle with two half-hitches.

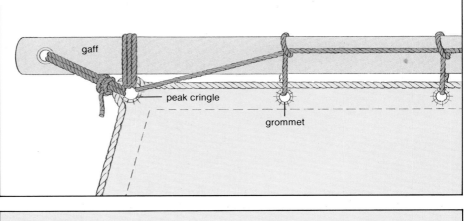

The foot of the sail is most often laced all the way around the boom, but sometimes it is bent instead onto a wooden rail—called a bending jackstay—that runs along the top of the boom. The foot of the sail is then held to the bending jackstay by individual robands, each of them anchored at a sail grommet with a tag hitch and secured to the bending jackstay with a square knot, as shown here.

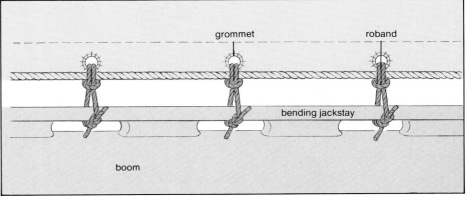

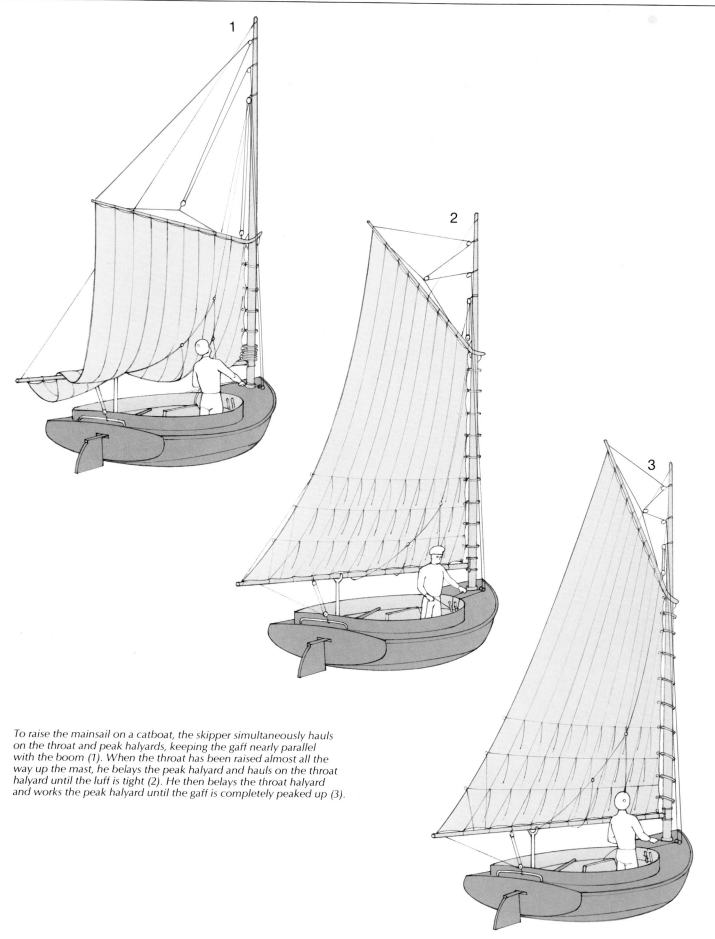

To raise the mainsail on a catboat, the skipper simultaneously hauls on the throat and peak halyards, keeping the gaff nearly parallel with the boom (1). When the throat has been raised almost all the way up the mast, he belays the peak halyard and hauls on the throat halyard until the luff is tight (2). He then belays the throat halyard and works the peak halyard until the gaff is completely peaked up (3).

Handling the Catboat

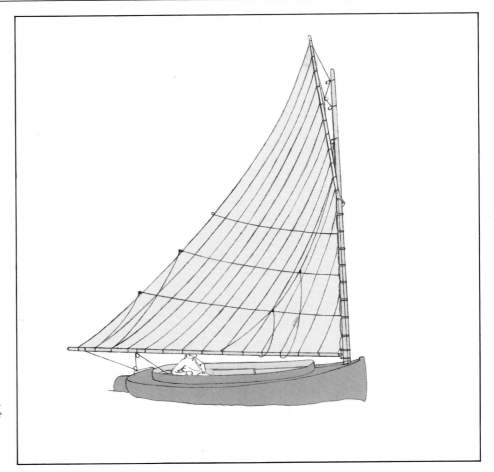

By adjusting the gaff's two halyards, the catboat sailor can achieve the proper set of his sail for maximum efficiency 'to windward. The throat halyard tightens the sail along the luff; the peak halyard adjusts the tension in the leech to remove any wrinkles that could interrupt the flow of the wind past the sail and thus reduce its driving force.

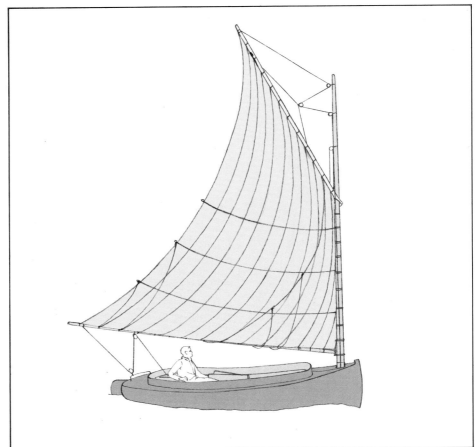

When sailing off the wind, the peak of the gaff is dropped slightly to slacken the leech, giving the sail more belly. The fuller sail holds more wind and thus extracts maximum pushing power. A gaff-rigged boat's ability to change the shape of its sail increases its efficiency both on and off the wind.

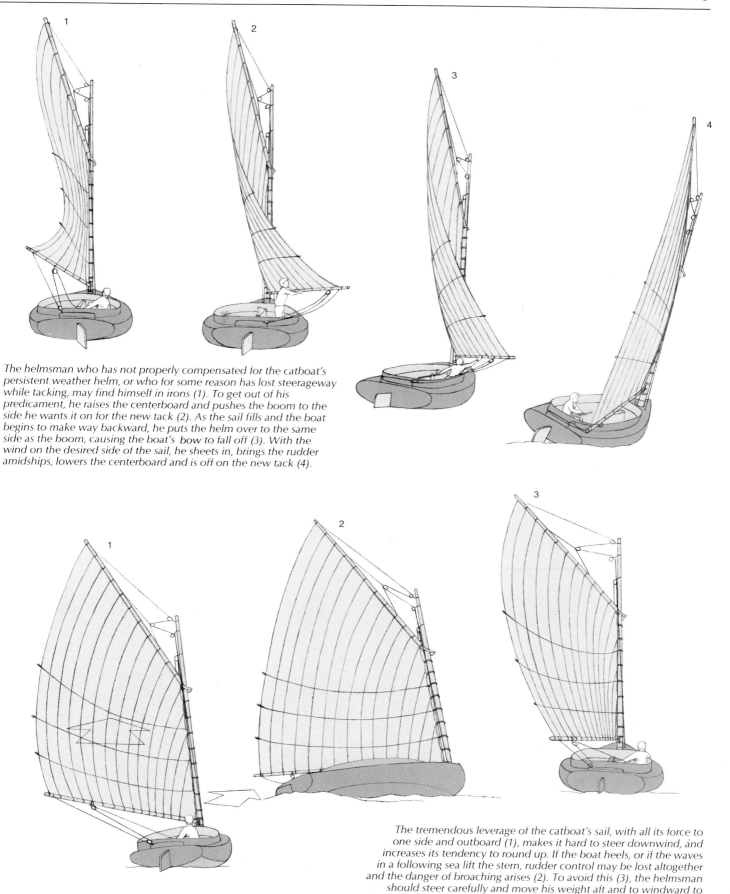

The helmsman who has not properly compensated for the catboat's persistent weather helm, or who for some reason has lost steerageway while tacking, may find himself in irons (1). To get out of his predicament, he raises the centerboard and pushes the boom to the side he wants it on for the new tack (2). As the sail fills and the boat begins to make way backward, he puts the helm over to the same side as the boom, causing the boat's bow to fall off (3). With the wind on the desired side of the sail, he sheets in, brings the rudder amidships, lowers the centerboard and is off on the new tack (4).

The tremendous leverage of the catboat's sail, with all its force to one side and outboard (1), makes it hard to steer downwind, and increases its tendency to round up. If the boat heels, or if the waves in a following sea lift the stern, rudder control may be lost altogether and the danger of broaching arises (2). To avoid this (3), the helmsman should steer carefully and move his weight aft and to windward to keep the boat balanced—even heeling slightly to weather if necessary. In a stiff breeze, when the threat of broaching is greater, he may also slack the peak and trim the mainsheet to spill wind.

Ways of Reducing Sail

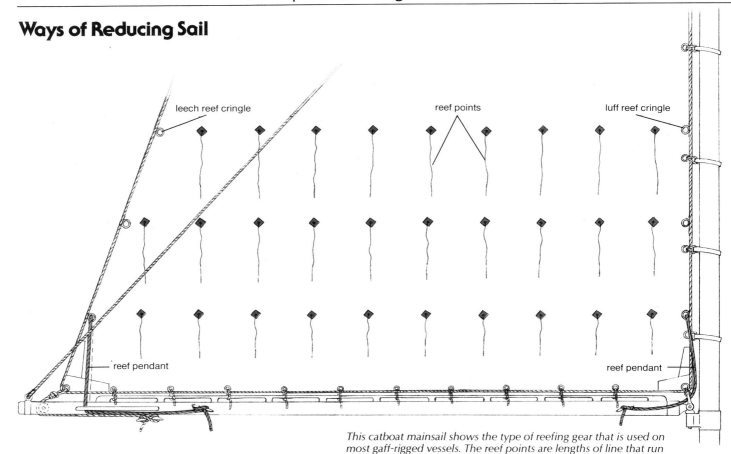

leech reef cringle

reef points

luff reef cringle

reef pendant

reef pendant

This catboat mainsail shows the type of reefing gear that is used on most gaff-rigged vessels. The reef points are lengths of line that run through grommets and hang down on either side of the sail; in heavy weather they are used to bend a reduced sail to the top of the boom. The cringles at the ends of each row act as grommets for tying down a new tack and clew. At least one set of pendants is attached to the cringles so that the sail can be lashed down in double-quick time.

Bonnets and Loose-footed Sails

Loose-footed sails—usually headsails—are occasionally rigged with a bonnet, a laced-on supplementary canvas panel that overlaps the foot of a moderate-sized sail and flies below it to enlarge sail area. When weather conditions require, a crewman can unlace the bonnet in a rapid series of steps without dropping the headsail. First he attaches a second pair of sheets to the clew cringle on the body of the sail (the companion tack cringle is kept permanently lashed at its proper elevation above the deck for just such reefing contingencies). He takes up on the new sheets until the strain transfers to them from the bonnet-hitched sheets; he then uncouples the slack sheets and the bolt ropes along the sail's leech and luff. Finally, he pulls on the after end of the lacing line (shown here in laced position). Like a rip cord, the line pulls free, loop releasing loop, and in a few seconds the surplus bonnet is detached. An alternative to the bonnet on loose-footed sails is standard reef points.

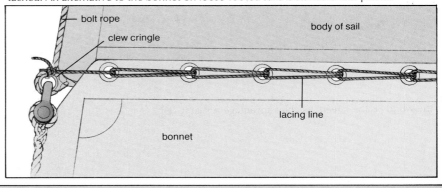

bolt rope

body of sail

clew cringle

lacing line

bonnet

To reduce canvas on a boomed sail, the reef pendant is threaded through the shackle on the gooseneck, the halyards eased to bring the reef points to rest on the boom, and the pendant tied down snug. If the sail is to be close-reefed, that is, reefed to its smallest size, sailors frequently reef at least one of the intermediary rows as well. Then, if the wind drops slightly, the skipper will have the option of breaking out the close reef without unfurling the entire sail.

Once the luff reef cringle is lashed, the seaman moves aft to set up the leech reef cringle, hauling it down through whatever fitting is most handy but preferably through a so-called reefing comb permanently fixed to the boom. The comb is an outhaul designed specifically for reefing pendants and it carries a series of holes along its length, each one positioned to give the proper purchase on the pendant above it. In hauling in on the pendant, the seaman must exercise care not to pull so tight that he stretches the sail.

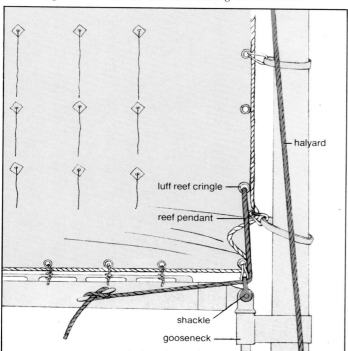

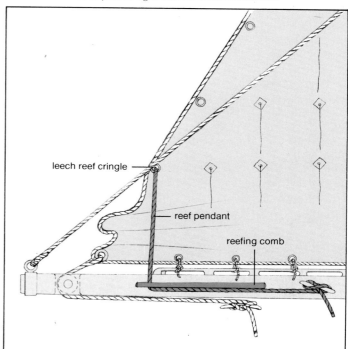

For the final steps the crewman moves again to the luff and starts furling the sail. Working on the windward side, he reaches under the boom, threads the leeward reef point under the foot of the sail, and draws it through. He ties the two in a slipped reef knot or square knot, taking care to compress the sail equally beneath each tie so that the strain of the wind against canvas will be fairly shared.

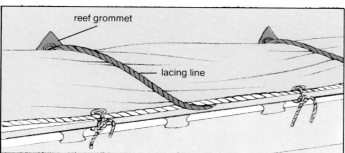

Reef lacing, an alternative to reef pointing, uses a continuous line that is inserted in the sail only after canvas has been reduced and the reef pendants hauled up tight. The crewman begins midway along the boom and works forward with one end of the line, circling it from each grommet to the underside of the sail foot, and through the back side of the next grommet, repeating the process until he reaches the gooseneck and can snub the line. He or another crew member laces the after portion of the sail in the same fashion. The technique takes more dexterity than reef pointing, particularly in rough seas or in the dark, but it produces a smoother, aerodynamically better fit of sail, which makes it a favored method aboard vintage racing craft.

The Popular Sloop

The classic rig that a pleasure sailor is most likely to encounter today is that of the traditional sloop. Fast and maneuverable upwind, easy to control on a reach or run, it was first popularized on workboats of medium size such as this Noank-type sloop, designed in the 1870s for fishing off the Connecticut coast. Besides its gaff-headed mainsail, it has a permanent bowsprit for setting one or more headsails.

The traditional rig requires elaborate standing rigging, including shrouds and stays of wire or rope wrapped in marline and canvas (opposite, below) and wire or chain bobstays. The shrouds are adjusted periodically with a system of deadeyes and lanyards (opposite, top), a task that is undertaken when the boat is in port.

The standing rigging of a Noank-type sloop includes two sets of rope shrouds attached to the mast near the crosstrees, and fitted with deadeyes near deck level. Each set is angled slightly aft to counteract the forward pull of the two stays that support the jib and staysail. A bobstay of either wire or chain prevents the bowsprit from being lifted upward when the headsails fill with wind.

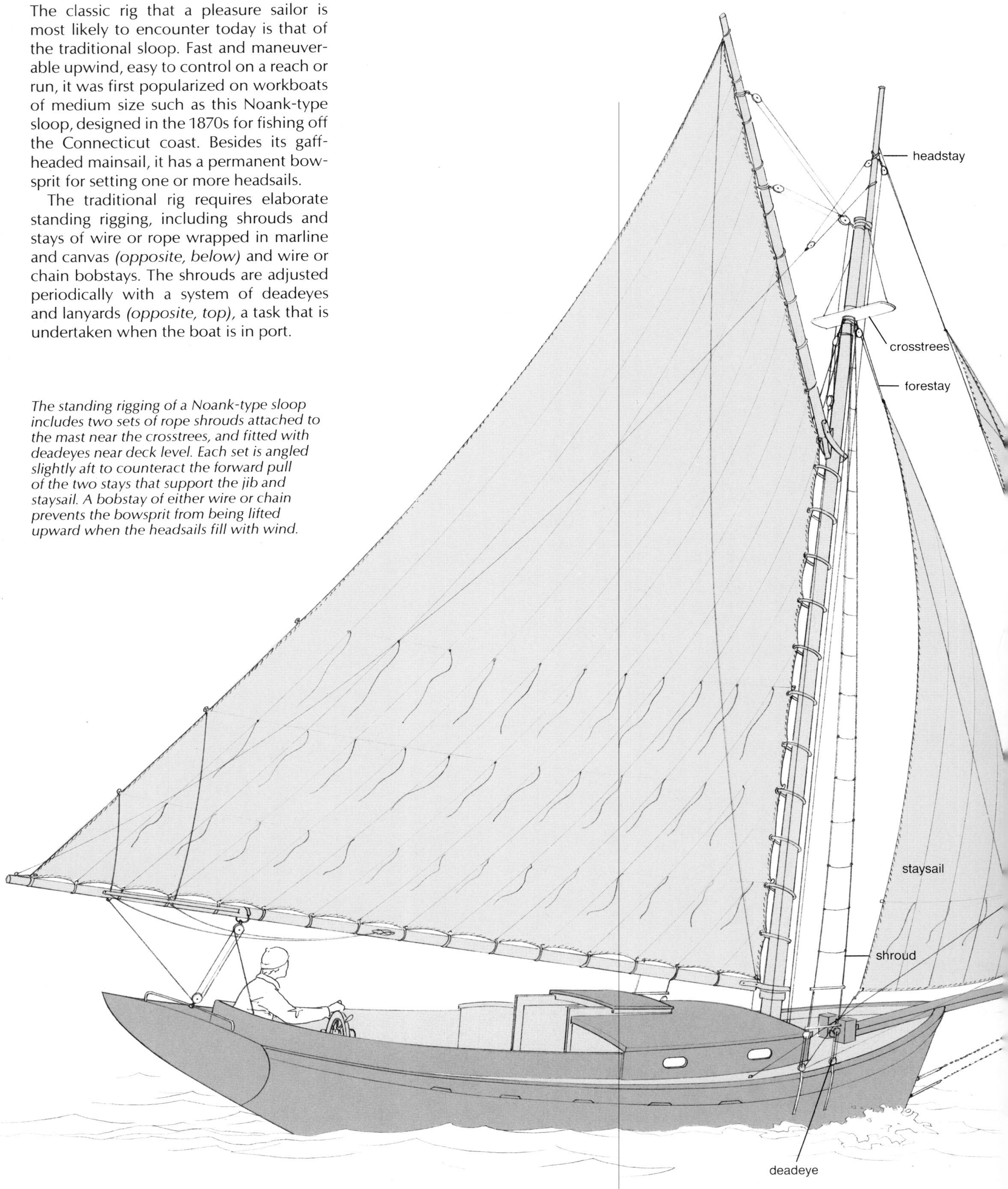

headstay

crosstrees

forestay

staysail

shroud

deadeye

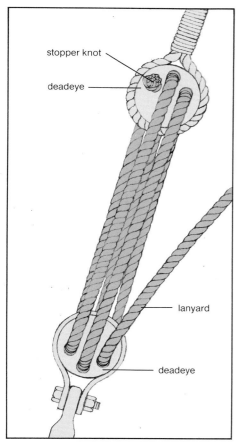

stopper knot

deadeye

lanyard

deadeye

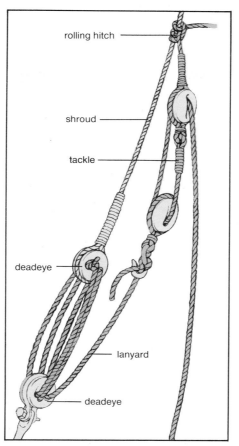

rolling hitch

shroud

tackle

deadeye

lanyard

deadeye

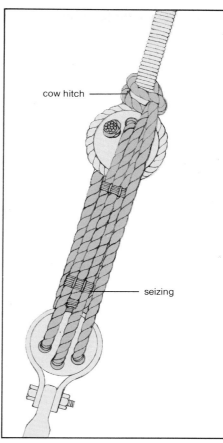

cow hitch

seizing

The deadeyes attached to the shrouds of classic sloops are the precursors of turnbuckles. To set them up, the rigger first lubricates the lanyard and the holes in each deadeye with grease so that he can thread them easily. Then, from inboard, he secures one end of the lanyard through the left hole in the upper deadeye with a stopper knot, and laces the working end through both of the deadeyes as shown above.

To draw up the lanyard and tighten the shroud, the sailor needs an auxiliary tackle. The tail of the tackle is secured to the shroud with a rolling hitch, and the hook is attached to the lanyard with a becket hitch, as shown. Then the sailor hauls down on the tackle and draws the lanyard up taut.

When the shroud has been given the proper tension, the sailor seizes the parts of the lanyard together to keep them from slipping. Then he unties the lanyard's end from the auxiliary tackle, runs it up around the shroud with a cow hitch, and brings it back parallel with the other parts. Finally, he seizes the working end of the lanyard, and finishes off with a waterproofing coat of tar.

jib

bobstay

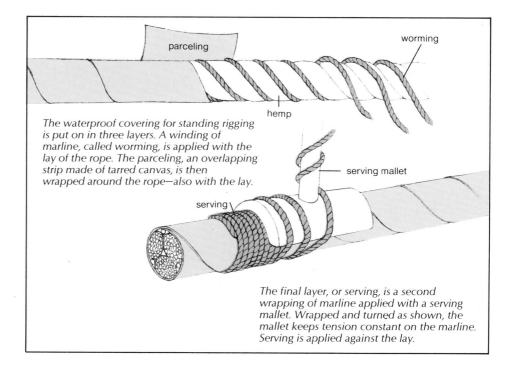

parceling

worming

hemp

serving mallet

serving

The waterproof covering for standing rigging is put on in three layers. A winding of marline, called worming, is applied with the lay of the rope. The parceling, an overlapping strip made of tarred canvas, is then wrapped around the rope—also with the lay.

The final layer, or serving, is a second wrapping of marline applied with a serving mallet. Wrapped and turned as shown, the mallet keeps tension constant on the marline. Serving is applied against the lay.

Options in Canvasing

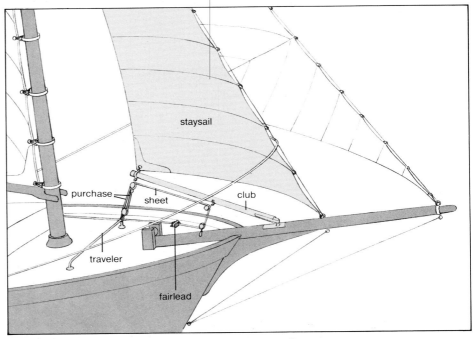

The staysail of a traditional sloop is often fitted with a wooden boom, or club, that lets the skipper change tacks without having to resheet the sail from one side of the boat to the other. The sheet runs from the end of the club through a purchase, which slides along a traveler when the boat tacks; it is then run aft through a fairlead, as here, to a convenient location in the cockpit. Often, the staysail is loose-footed like this one, rather than laced to the club. The loose-fitted rig gives the sail maximum driving power, and allows the skipper to adjust the sail's camber according to wind conditions.

A Sloop with Seasonal Sails

The New York sloop, a swift fishing boat that worked New York Harbor in the mid-19th Century, sported a rig for summer and one for winter. From late spring through early fall, the craft carried a typical working sloop's gaff-headed mainsail and jib. But for blustery winter weather, the skipper removed the jib and plank bowsprit and re-stepped the mast forward—transforming the sloop into a catboat.

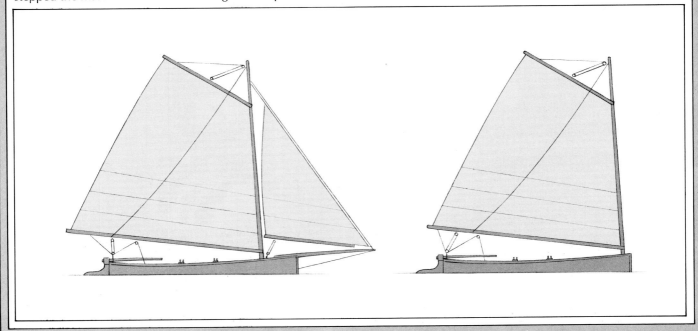

A sloop's multiple sail plan provides tremendous versatility for adjusting sail area to various wind strengths—particularly when the boat carries double headsails like this Noank-type craft. In light to moderate winds, the skipper normally flies his full complement of working sails—jib, staysail and unreefed mainsail, as shown below.

In a fresh breeze of 17 knots or more, the skipper starts to reduce sail by striking his jib. If the wind begins gusting up from 21 to 27 knots, his large mainsail will more than likely produce a strong weather helm, and he will have to tie in a first reef, as shown, to balance his rig.

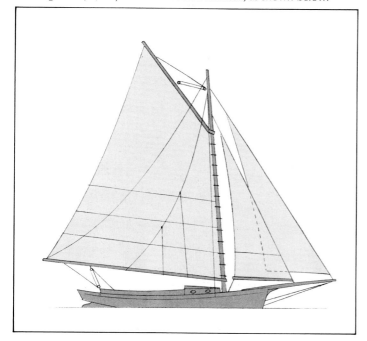
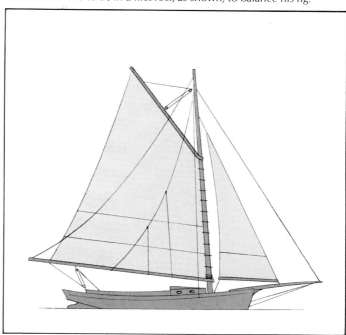

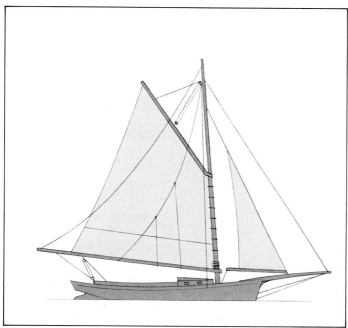
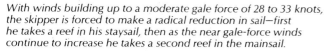
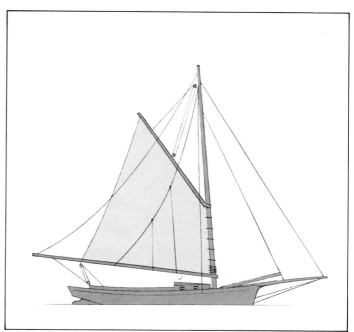

With winds building up to a moderate gale force of 28 to 33 knots, the skipper is forced to make a radical reduction in sail—first he takes a reef in his staysail, then as the near gale-force winds continue to increase he takes a second reef in the mainsail.

In a 40-knot gale, the skipper takes a final close reef in his main. With any significant increase—winds of 48 knots or more, say—he will have to strike his staysail and ride out the storm with his triple-reefed main sheeted in hard and his tiller lashed slightly to leeward. This way he can heave to with his bow into the wind and keep forward motion through the water to an absolute minimum.

A familiar sight along the New England coast in years past, the pinky is a type of small fishing schooner built principally in and around Essex, Massachusetts. The boat is characterized by its "pinked"—pointed —stern, a feature that makes it seaworthy and comfortable in deep water. Its rig is essentially that of all fore-and-aft schooners, though it is simpler than many in that it carries a main topmast but no fore topmast.

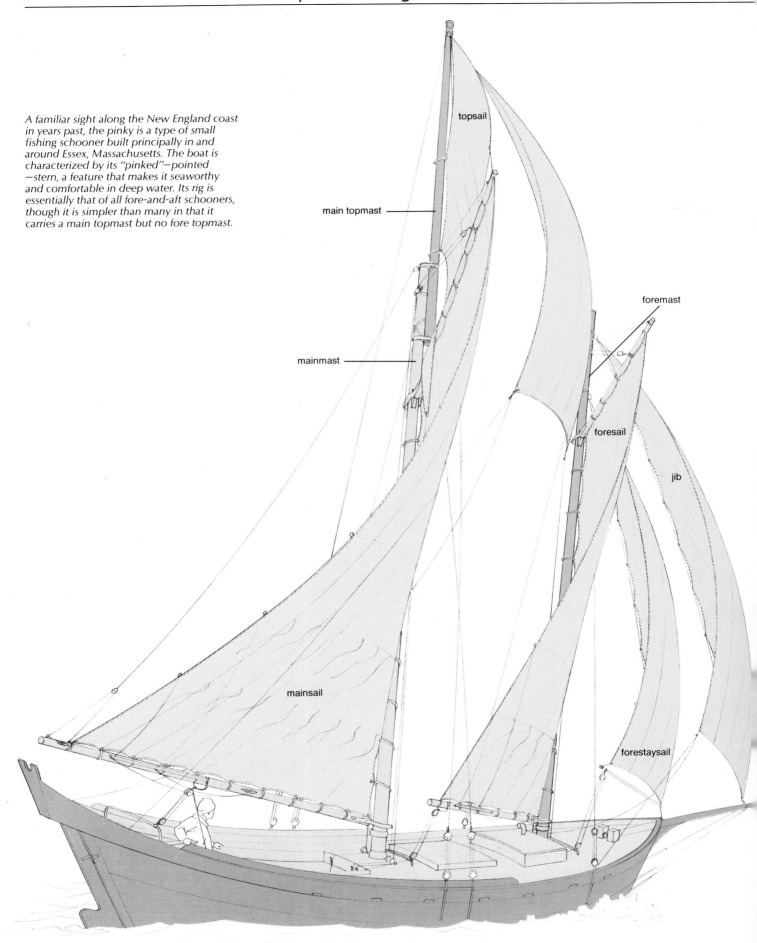

topsail

main topmast

foremast

mainmast

foresail

jib

mainsail

forestaysail

The Versatile Schooner

The New England pinky at left is one of many variations on the gaff-rigged two-masted schooner, a boat type developed in America in the early 1700s for fishing, smuggling, piloting larger boats and carrying cargo between coastal towns.

Today, long after the schooner has lost its usefulness as a workboat, a few yacht designers have continued to build pleasure boats along its honest lines, and some of the old workboats have been converted to private recreational use.

With a foremast, a mainmast, one or two topmasts, and a large assortment of heavy and light sails, the schooner rig can be tailored to sail effectively in practically any wind condition. In summer, for example, one of the schooner's most notable features is frequently a topsail, a triangular sail raised on the main topmast, which can take full advantage of any breezes aloft. In spring and fall, however, the conservative skipper is likely to keep his topsails stowed. A schooner may also have a choice of fisherman's staysails in a couple of sizes and weights to spread high between its two masts.

Altogether, a working schooner of 50 feet or so can crowd on as many as six sails with a complement of as few as four experienced hands. If the weather is threatening or if some of the crew are busy at other duties, the skipper can reduce sail to the basics—mainsail, foresail, and two headsails—and reduce the deck crew to as few as two. The standing and running rigging for so many sails is naturally complex; it calls upon all the aids to hoisting and pulling available to old-time sailors. Some of these aids are shown at right.

The task of setting canvas on a large boat requires some cooperative tactics for energy conservation. Here, two crewmen have hauled the hefty foresail up, keeping the gaff roughly parallel with the boom, as far as easy hand-over-hand hauling will take it; now, the peak man, having belayed his halyard, comes around to help set up the throat halyard. His companion pulls the halyard out from the mast, bracing his foot for extra leverage; he will walk the slack that he has gained back to the mast while the other man takes it in. The process is repeated until the luff is taut. The two then sweat up the peak.

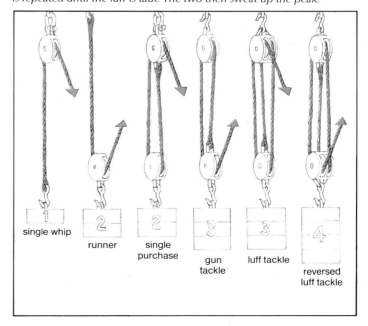

The tackles that make sheets and halyards work vary, depending upon the mechanical advantages or purchases they provide. The purchase is determined by the number of parts of a line leading to and from a moving block; thus the single whip on a stationary block provides no power advantage but is used to change the height and direction of the force as in a simple jib halyard. Reversed, the same block produces two pounds of force for every pound of pulling effort. A few other tackles are shown with their names and purchase factors. (The actual purchase is somewhat less, owing to friction.)

single whip — runner — single purchase — gun tackle — luff tackle — reversed luff tackle

Sails for a Summer Day

On American schooners, the topsail is usually raised and trimmed to windward, after the main is set, using four lines running to the deck: a halyard run through a fitting in the topmast; a sheet rove from the clew through a block on the main gaff and then through a jewel block (on a pendant hanging from the gaff jaws); a tack line; and a line to control the luff. Here, the luff is attached to a leader which circles the topmast in an eyesplice. The fall is rove through cringles on the luff before the sail is raised. The lower part of the luff is cut away to avoid chafing against the mast and rigging. As the sail is hoisted, the eyesplice rides up the topmast with it; when the sail is set, the halyard and tack line are secured and the leader tightened to bring the sail snug to the mast. If a short tack is necessary, the topsail is left on the side where it was originally set. For longer tacks it is brought down to the deck and reset on the new windward side.

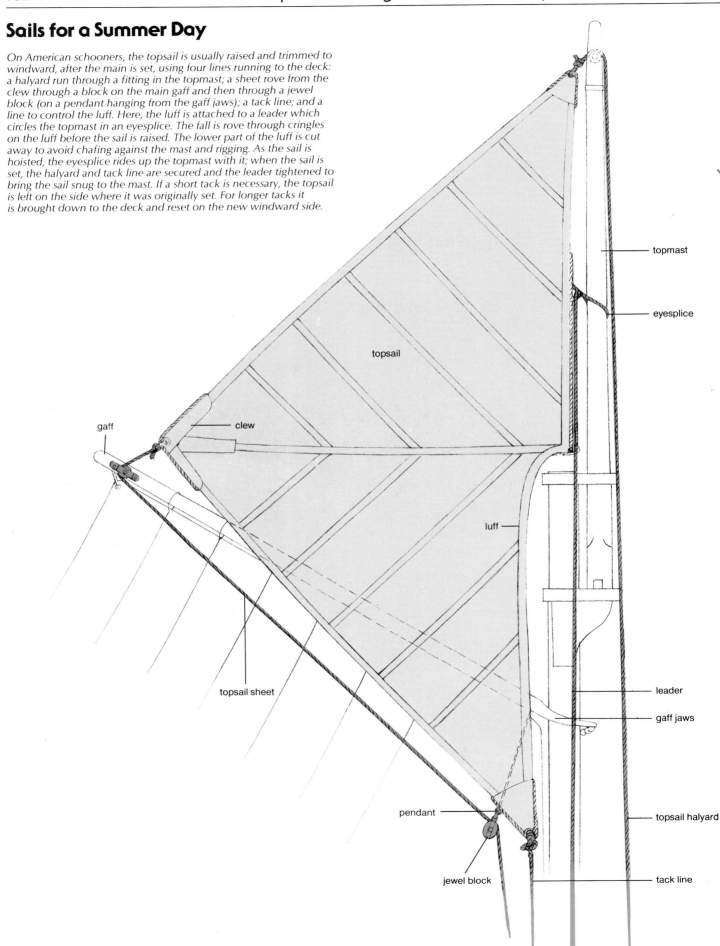

topmast

eyesplice

topsail

gaff

clew

luff

topsail sheet

leader

gaff jaws

pendant

topsail halyard

jewel block

tack line

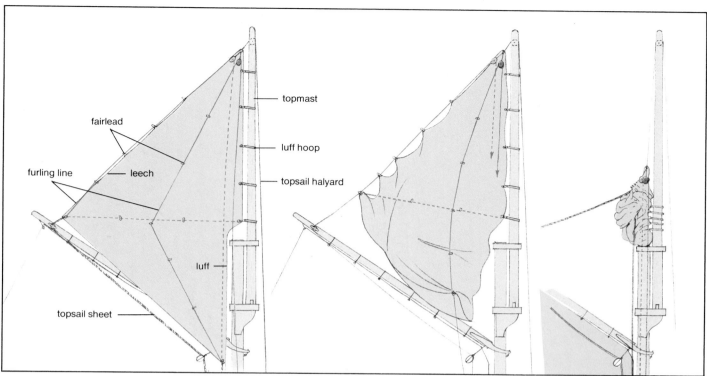

topmast

luff hoop

topsail halyard

fairlead

furling line   leech

luff

topsail sheet

Some topsails stay on all season and are set by a furling technique. The topsail's sheet, halyard and tack line operate in a conventional manner; in this example, the difference lies in a pair of furling lines (blue), rove, as shown, through cringles or fairleads on the sail. To strike the sail the tack line and sheet are released and the furling lines hauled in from the deck, until the sail forms a ball. The halyard is then lowered until the sail rests against the topmast base.

The Racer's Edge

In their quest for speed, designers of racing yachts in the late 19th Century experimented constantly to increase the total amount of canvas a vessel could fly. Typical of their daring excesses was the rig of the 95-foot schooner *Corona (right)* equipped with two topsails—a club topsail on her mainmast, and a gollywobbler flying between her two spars.

The club topsail (or jackyard topsail) first appeared in the 1850s. Its distinctive feature was a yard, laced to the after end of the topsail's foot, which made possible extending its clew beyond the limits imposed by the mainsail gaff on a conventional topsail (such as that on *Corona's* foremast). As an extra bonus, the additional canvas gained by this device was frequently overlooked in the rating formulas used in early racing.

Setting and tacking a club topsail required skillful handling on deck and aloft. *Corona's* gollywobbler also made extravagant demands on the crew. An oversized version of the quadrilateral fisherman's staysail *(page 154),* it substantially overlapped the main, and therefore had to be taken down and totally rerigged with each change of tack.

A Change of Sails at Sea

A fisherman's staysail is run up between the masts on halyards, which are rigged to straddle the spring stay connecting the two masts. To set the staysail, the crew hitch the leeward falls of the halyards to the sail's peak and throat, a sheet to the clew and a line to the tack. They reeve the sheet through a lead on the main boom and down to the deck. The crewmen now haul on the windward halyards and when the sail is topped they snub the tack line and trim the sheet. For a long tack the staysail must be reset.

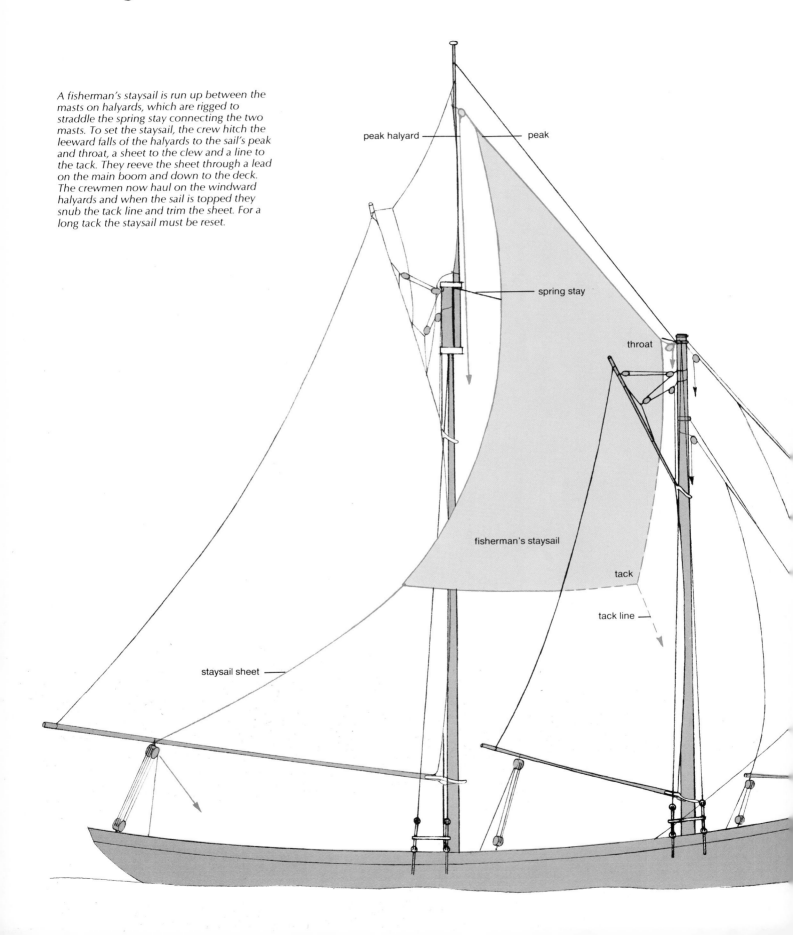

peak halyard

peak

spring stay

throat

fisherman's staysail

tack

tack line

staysail sheet

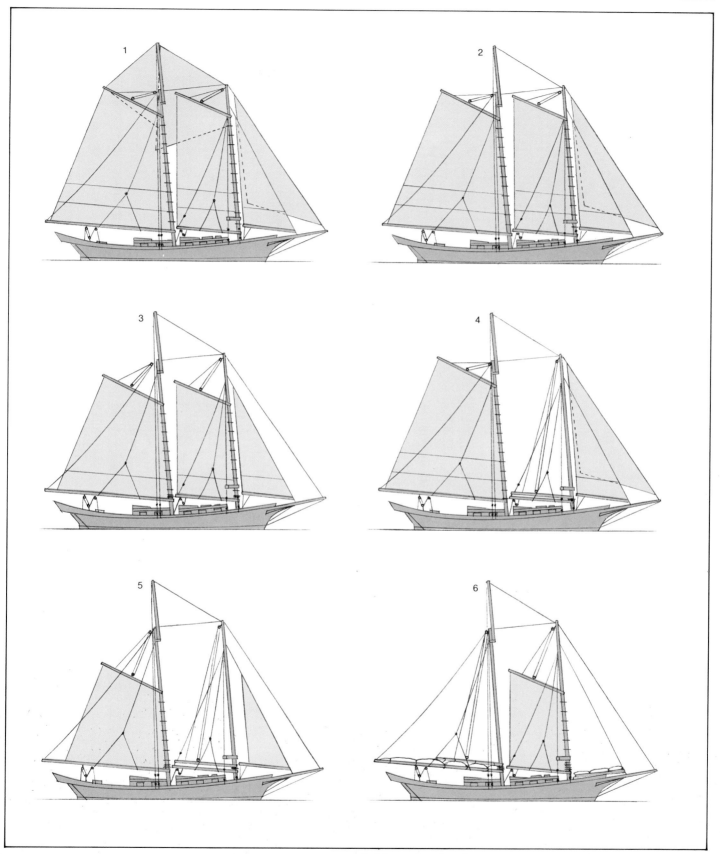

In fair weather, the schooner may carry a topsail (1) and fisherman's staysail (represented in part by dotted lines). But when heading into wind and waves, the lofty sails are stowed (2). As wind rises, the first reef is taken in both the main and foresail (3) or the foresail is doused (4); a close reef is taken in the mainsail and the headsails reduced (5) until the boat is proceeding under reefed foresail alone (6).

THE SPORTING WORLD OF LOG CANOES

Nearly every summer weekend on Chesapeake Bay, the world's tippiest sailboats meet in regattas that are as much struggles to avoid capsizing as they are contests of speed. The craft are 27-to-35-foot canoes built of logs and carrying fully three times as much sail area as most other boats of their length. In order to balance such enormous spreads of canvas, the vessels' crew members must scurry in and out on long planks that they shove six or seven feet over the windward rail. At the same time the crew must tack, jibe, bail and hoist additional sails in a constant scramble of activity.

Just steering a log canoe calls for precise, coordinated teamwork. Since the sails overpower the relatively small rudder, a log canoe responds sluggishly to the helm. Before a skipper can change course, the crew must adjust the trim of the sheets so that the sails help turn the boat.

These temperamental craft, which have been raced all along Maryland's Eastern Shore since about 1840, are descendants of Indian canoes made from single, hollowed-out logs. The Chesapeake's first colonial settlers refined construction by fastening several logs together side by side, and then shaping and hollowing them. They built up the topsides with planking and added masts and a bowsprit to support a set of working sails.

The colonists used the boats to gather oysters from Chesapeake Bay; once loaded, the oystermen would race to shore to sell their catch. Before long log-canoe racing for sport alone caught on, and pleasure boatmen began ordering up canoes designed for competition, extending the rig and piling on sails to catch every bit of the usually light Chesapeake breeze.

As it has evolved, the classic Chesapeake Bay canoe carries two masts, each supporting a four-sided sail. The aftermost edges of these two sails are laced to short spars called clubs, and are held out from the mast by horizontal sprits—locally pronounced "spreet."

Besides the four-sided main and foresail, each canoe carries a huge jib laced to a horizontal boom that runs parallel to the bowsprit. The jib is set flying—that is, it is kept aloft by the halyard alone, since there is no forestay on which to fasten the leading edge. Augmenting this basic rig, the canoeists may add an array of square and triangular topsails.

Many of the canoes racing today are close to 100 years old and have been handed down in the same family from generation to generation. To keep these craft sailing, the owners must be lavish in their love and attention. At the beginning of each new season, the boats are thoroughly overhauled—logs and planking probed for dry rot, and any faulty members replaced. Spars must be periodically scraped and revarnished, hulls repainted. One working wife who bought an old work canoe for $50 estimates her entire salary has gone for its upkeep.

Whenever an old canoe is restored or a new one built, each detail of construction follows rigorous guidelines that are set down by the Chesapeake Bay Log Sailing Canoe Association, which conducts the races. The regattas themselves—like the season-opening scramble shown on the following pages—have scarcely changed over the years. The boats go around a triangular course in a set of three handicap races, with time allowances given on the basis of length and beam.

Unlike many other types of day races, which have become highly technical athletic events, log-canoe races have retained a carefully nurtured aura of informality. They are primarily family affairs: one skipper, who owns three canoes, musters a total of 27 relatives and friends each weekend to help sail them. And though dunkings are frequent and fame is fleeting in the topsy-turvy world of the log-canoe racer, recruiting a crew is rarely difficult. For the experience of maneuvering these intriguing craft around the Bay under their enormous cumulus of sail is one of the most challenging and delightful experiences in pleasure sailing.

With her foresail freshly hoisted, a log canoe en route to the season's first race ghosts past a sister canoe beached in the reeds of a Maryland inlet.

A gang of Chesapeake sailors prepares for the start of a new racing
season by upending a 33-foot log canoe that had been turned bottom-
up for work on the hull. Built in 1892, the canoe is six inches thick in
some areas along the keel, weighs approximately 3,500 pounds and
will require a tow truck to lift it onto a trailer for launching.

After launching a canoe, crew members fit the foot of the foremast
into its step; they will then walk the mast forward to bring it vertical.
The mast will be held in place with wooden wedges and rigged with
a single pair of shrouds—the only standing rigging in the entire boat.

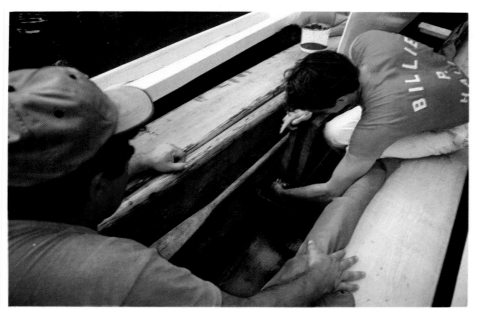

To seal up minor leaks in a newly launched canoe, a crewman applies a temporary caulking of thick grease around the centerboard trunk. Since the canoes are hauled ashore off-season, the wood dries out and the seams in the hull tend to open up —an occurrence that sparks considerable badinage among rival crews, who routinely pronounce their opponent's craft unseaworthy. A teaspoon of grease, daubed into cracks, stems the leaking until the wood has a chance to swell, closing the seams.

A deckhand hoists the 500-square-foot foresail of the 73-year-old Billie P. Hall, one of the Bay's fastest canoes. When the halyard has been made fast, the crewman standing next to the mast will haul on the sprit line, which runs from the forward end of the sprit partway up the mast. This line simultaneously raises the sprit and forces it aft, thus flattening the sail for upwind work.

Rigged and fully manned, the Billie P. Hall heads out smartly for some brief prerace practice in tacking, the trickiest maneuver in log-canoe sailing. As the canoe moves along on port tack, six crew members balance on three movable hiking boards wedged under the lee rail. Another crewman, perched aft of the helmsman on an outrigger that projects over the stern, controls the main sheet, while a man next to the bow trims the jib.

The tack begins as the skipper turns the craft head to wind, while the six hikers scurry inboard, lifting the hiking boards out from under the rail and then heaving them across toward the new windward side. One crewman pauses to release the foresail sheet and makes ready to retrim it on the other side.

After tucking the boards under the leeward rail, the six hikers climb out to weather as the sails begin to fill on the new tack. An agile and experienced crew can bring about a log canoe in less than 20 seconds.

The maneuver completed, all hands lean out to weather to keep the canoe from capsizing on the new tack. To minimize strain on the rig —and to avoid exhausting the crew—most helmsmen restrict tacking to several practice turns before the starting gun.

Just after the starting gun for the first race, the fleet heads toward the weather mark; two of the boats fly small triangular sails called kites from their foremasts. The handicapping rules for log-canoe racing place no limitations on sail area, so extra sails—kites, square sails and staysails—may be hoisted at any time. Kites, many of which are converted Sunfish sails, are often carried throughout a race. Square sails are usually saved for leeward legs.

The canoe Jay Dee sails a slow leg before the wind with her foresail and mainsail spread wing-and-wing, and hiking boards slung athwartships. The hikers sit inboard to balance the boat, while the skipper and one crew member peer aft, keeping an eye out for competition and for puffs of wind.

The crew of a capsized canoe, which overturned when the helmsman rounded the first mark faster than the sheets could be eased, watches ruefully as a rival sails by. Since a capsized canoe fills completely with water, it is almost impossible to right and bail dry. It must instead be towed ashore by a rescue craft, which will also take aboard sails, spars and other loose gear—in this case empty beer cans floating on top of the jib.

The first-place cannon fires as Island Bird, carrying a kite emblazoned with an osprey, crosses the finish line. Only 27 feet 4 inches long, Island Bird, the smallest of all the Chesapeake's racing log canoes, sailed this race so smartly that she managed to finish two minutes ahead of her nearest rival with no need to resort to her time handicap.

The *Billie P. Hall* heads back to the starting
line for the next race of the regatta, her crew
moving out on the boards, as a gust of wind
catches the vessel's enormous canopy of sail.

Associations

The following organizations are excellent sources of information on the repair, restoration and maintenance of classic boats. Most produce newsletters or quarterly publications on these subjects, and many of them stage annual classic-boat shows or regattas.

Ancient Mariners Sailing Society
Doug Smith, Commodore
5144 Rincon Street
San Diego, California 92115

The Antique and Classic Boat Society, Inc.
Ray Nelson, President
P.O. Box 831
Lake George, New York 12845

Antique Boat & Yacht Club
Alen Sands York, Commodore
1040 Avenue of the Americas
New York, New York 10018

Antique Boat Society, Inc.
Adm. E. R. Welles, President
Manset Post Office, Maine 04656

Antique Outboard Motor Club
W. J. Webb, Historian
2560 North 97th Street
Wauwatosa, Wisconsin 53226

Chris-Craft Antique Boat Club
Howard Hallas, Secretary-Treasurer
P.O. Box 1065
Long Boat Key, Florida 33548

Classic Yacht Association
Jim Gerig, Commodore
4215 Sherman Oaks Avenue
Sherman Oaks, California 91403

The Classic Yacht Club of America, Inc.
519 Worcester Road
Towson, Maryland 21204

The Elco Club
Richard Cook, Commodore
12 W. Main Street
Mystic, Connecticut 06355

Master Mariners Benevolent Association
William E. Vaughan, Commodore
17 Embarcadero Cove
Oakland, California 94606

Master Mariners Association of Puget Sound
Capt. Robert L. Riddle, President
c/o Sea/Land Service, Inc.
P.O. Box 3045
Seattle, Washington 98114

Northwest Steam Society
John E. Granquist, Chairman
P.O. Box 9727
Seattle, Washington 98109

Puget Sound Live Steamers
Everett A. Arnes
1052 Sterling Road
Sedro Woolley, Washington 98284

Richardson Boat Owner's Association
William Lindquist, President
2046 Lake Road
Ontario, New York 14519

Schooner Association of America
Bill Druitt, Commodore
529 West Santa Clara Avenue
Santa Ana, California 92706

Traditional Wooden Boat Society
Dick Wagner
2770 Westlake North
Seattle, Washington 98109

Wooden Hull Owners' Association
4700 East 7th Street
Long Beach, California 90804

Museums

Among the many institutions offering collections of restored classic boats, lines plans, artifacts, and books relating to classic boats, are the following notable examples, with some of their special offerings also cited.

Adirondack Museum
Blue Mountain Lake, New York 12812
—Adirondack guide boats, North Woods boats, canoes, kayaks, sailboats and steamboats.

Bath Marine Museum
963 Washington Street
Bath, Maine 04530
—Apprenticeship program in small-boat building and restoration, models, tools, instruments.

Chesapeake Bay Maritime Museum
P.O. Box 636
St. Michaels, Maryland 21663
—Small-boat building program, shipyard for restoration work, small boats, ship models, marine engines and instruments, library, paintings.

Columbia River Maritime Museum
16th and Exchange Streets
Astoria, Oregon 97103
—Columbia River craft, models, whaling artifacts, instruments, paintings, prints, photographs.

Francis Russell Hart Nautical Museum
77 Massachusetts Avenue
Cambridge, Massachusetts 02139
—Ship, yacht and engine models; extensive library; substantial collection of lines plans; photographs and paintings.

Great Lakes Historical Society Museum
480 Main Street
Vermilion, Ohio 44089
—Ship models, marine engines, artifacts, paintings, photographs, library.

Greenfield Village & Henry Ford Museum
Dearborn, Michigan 48121
—Small craft, marine engines, artifacts.

The Mariners' Museum
Museum Drive
Newport News, Virginia 23606
—Extensive library, international marine artifacts, models and exhibits of small craft in the water.

The Maritime Museum Association of San Diego
1306 North Harbor Drive
San Diego, California 92101
—*Star of India*, a three-masted merchant ship, and the steam yacht *Medea* in floating exhibits; ship models; artifacts.

Mystic Seaport, Inc.
Greenmanville Avenue
Mystic, Connecticut 06355
—Major collections of craft, large and small; artifacts; paintings and prints; library; research facilities; publications and lines plans for sale.

Nantucket Whaling Museum
Nantucket, Massachusetts 02554
—Fine whaling collection, ship models, artifacts, library.

Peabody Museum of Salem
161 Essex Street
Salem, Massachusetts 01970
—Ship models, ships' tools and instruments, photographs, paintings.

Penobscot Marine Museum
Church Street
Searsport, Maine 04974
—Collection of Maine boats, artifacts, ship models, tools, paintings, prints.

Philadelphia Maritime Museum
321 Chestnut Street
Philadelphia, Pennsylvania 19106
—Major library, artifacts, ship models, prints and paintings, barkentine *Gazela Primeiro* nearby.

San Francisco Maritime Museum
Foot of Polk Street
San Francisco, California 94109
—Ship models, artifacts, photographs, paintings.

Smithsonian Institution
National Museum of History and Technology
Constitution Avenue at 14th Street
Washington, D.C. 20560
—The National Watercraft Collection of 200-odd models, Howard Chapelle's invaluable library of lines plans.

South Street Seaport Museum
16 Fulton Street
New York, New York 10038
—Workboats, large and small, some undergoing restoration at pierside;

artifacts; ship models; research library with photographs and prints; largest collection of maritime publications for sale.

Strawbery Banke
P.O. Box 300
Hancock and Washington Streets
Portsmouth, New Hampshire 03801
—Traditional wooden small craft built in a workshop as part of a historic restoration project.

Thousand Islands Museum
Thousand Islands Shipyard Museum
Clayton, New York 13624
—Neighboring facilities exhibiting St. Lawrence River skiffs, canoes, artifacts, antique powerboats and engines.

Bibliography

General

Ansel, Willits D., *Restoration of the Smack Emma C. Berry at Mystic Seaport 1969-1971.* The Marine Historical Association, Incorporated, 1973.

Ashley, Clifford W., *The Ashley Book of Knots.* Doubleday & Company, Inc., 1944.

Bloomster, Edgar L., *Sailing and Small Craft Down the Ages.* United States Naval Institute, 1940.

Brewington, M. V., *Chesapeake Bay Log Canoes and Bugeyes.* Cornell Maritime Press, Inc., 1963.

Chapelle, Howard I.:
American Sailing Craft. International Marine Publishing Company, 1975.
American Small Sailing Craft. W. W. Norton & Company, Inc., 1951.
Boatbuilding. W. W. Norton & Company, Inc., 1969.
The National Watercraft Collection, Second Edition. Smithsonian Institution Press and International Marine Publishing Company, 1976.
Yacht Designing and Planning, Revised Edition. W. W. Norton & Company, Inc., 1936.

Chapman, Charles F., and F. W. Horenburger, eds., *Complete Designs for 44 Modern Boats.* Motor Boating, 1941.

Culler, R. D., *Skiffs and Schooners.* International Marine Publishing Company, 1974.

Day, Cyrus Lawrence, *The Art of Knotting and Splicing,* Third Edition. Naval Institute Press, 1970.

Gillmer, Thomas C., *Working Watercraft.* International Marine Publishing Company, 1972.

Graumont, Raoul, and John Hensel, *Encyclopedia of Knots and Fancy Rope Work,* Fourth Edition. Cornell Maritime Press, Inc., 1952.

Guthorn, Peter J., *The Sea Bright Skiff and Other Jersey Shore Boats.* Rutgers University Press, 1971.

Herreshoff, L. Francis:
Capt. Nat Herreshoff, The Wizard of Bristol. Sheridan House, 1953.
Sensible Cruising Designs. International Marine Publishing Company, 1973.
The Common Sense of Yacht Design. Caravan-Maritime Books, 1973.

Hornell, James, *Water Transport.* David & Charles, 1970.

Landstrom, Bjorn, *The Ship.* Doubleday & Company, Inc., 1961.

Leather, John, *Gaff Rig.* International Marine Publishing Company, 1976.

Leavens, John M., ed., *The Catboat Book.* International Marine Publishing Company, 1973.

Lewis, John, *Restoring Vintage Boats.* International Marine Publishing Company, 1975.

O'Brien, Conor:
Deep-Water Yacht Rig. Oxford University Press, 1948.
The Practical Man's Cruiser. Oxford University Press, 1940.
Yacht Gear and Gadgets. Oxford University Press, 1946.

Smith, Hervey Garrett, *The Marlinspike Sailor.* John de Graff, Inc., 1971.

Stackpole, Edouard A., and James Kleinschmidt, "Small Craft at Mystic Seaport." No. 36. The Marine Historical Association, Inc., 1959.

Steward, Robert M., *Boatbuilding Manual.* International Marine Publishing Company, 1970.

Traung, Jan-Olaf, ed., *Fishing Boats of the World.* The Fishing News—Arthur J. Heighway Publications Ltd., 1955.

Tryckare, Tre, *The Lore of Ships.* Holt, Rinehart and Winston, 1963.

Underhill, Harold A., *Masting and Rigging the Clipper Ship & Ocean Carrier.* Brown, Son and Ferguson, Ltd., 1946.

Museum Directories

America's Historic Ships, Replicas & Restorations. Arco Publishing Company, Inc., New York, 1975.

Nautical Museum Directory, Third Edition. Quadrant Press, Inc., New York, 1973.

Repertory of Maritime Museums and Collections. National Maritime Museum, Antwerp, Belgium, 1966-1969.

Periodicals

Antique Boating, Ray Nelson, Editor, Cleverdale, New York.

National Fisherman, Camden, Maine.

The Wooden Boat, Jonathan Wilson, Editor and Publisher, North Brooksville, Maine.

Glossary

Apex line A line representing the deepest point in a rabbet.

Apron A curved timber, fastened to the after side of the stem to provide a surface to which the forward ends of the side planking fasten.

Backbone A hull's central fore-and-aft structural component comprised of its keel, stem and stern members.

Ballast keel A heavy keel, usually of cast lead or iron, that lowers the hull's center of gravity and thus increases resistance to heeling.

Base line A fore-and-aft line drawn below the keel in lines plans and loftings from which heights to various points on the hull are measured.

Batten A thin strip of wood used to fair the lines of a boat throughout the construction process; also, a strip of wood inserted in the sail to shape it; also, certain long thin timbers used in hull construction, as in batten seam planking.

Bearding line A line representing the inner edge of a rabbet.

Becket A loop, eye or grommet; the eye in the strap of a block to which a line can be attached.

Belay To secure a line to a cleat or pin.

Bend To fasten, as a sail to a spar or stay.

Bending jackstay A rope, iron rod or strip of wood attached to a spar and onto which a sail is bent.

Billethead An ornamental, curved stem piece, above the cutwater and below the bowsprit, that ends in a scroll or fiddlehead.

Binnacle Housing of the compass.

Bitt A post fixed on or through a deck for securing mooring lines and towlines.

Block A wood or metal shell enclosing one or more sheaves, through which lines are led.

Bobstay A heavy wire, rope or iron rod that runs from the end of the bowsprit to the stem to counteract the lifting strain of the forestay.

Body plan In a lines plan, the sectional view of the hull as seen from the stem and stern.

Boltrope A rope sewed to the edge of a sail to strengthen it against tearing.

Bonnet A strip of canvas laced across the bottom of a loose-footed sail to increase its area in fair weather. It is unlaced to reduce sail.

Bowsprit A spar that projects forward from a boat's stem to extend its headsails.

Brail On a loose-footed sail, a horizontal line running from the afterleech to the luff, usually spliced to a line that runs down the mast. Several brails are used to gather the sail in to the mast for furling.

Breasthook A triangular-shaped, horizontal knee fitted abaft the stem; used to tie the bows together.

Bridle A span of rope secured at both ends; used to distribute the pulling power of any line attached to its bight.

Broach A boat is said to broach when it swerves and heels dangerously, so that the hull turns broadside to the waves and is in danger of capsizing or foundering.

Broad plank One of several strakes above the garboard strake.

Butt block A backing piece used to strengthen the joint where the sections of a strake butt together.

Buttocks In a lines plan, the contour lines that represent vertical, lengthwise slices through the surface of the hull.

Cabin sole The floor of the cabin.

Camber The convex curvature, as of a sail or deck.

Capstan A vertical drum, revolving on a spindle, used for hoisting or hauling.

Carlin A fore-and-aft structural member of the deck framing used to support the sides of deck openings such as cockpits.

Carvel planking A planking method in which the strakes are joined edge to edge, forming a smooth hull surface.

Ceiling An inner planking laid over the frames inside the hull for added strength.

Center line In a lines plan, the line that represents the longitudinal, vertical plane that divides the hull in half, and from which all half-breadths are measured.

Center of effort A theoretical point on a boat's sail plan that represents the center of wind forces on the sails.

Chine The angled intersection between a boat's topsides and bottom.

Chine log An inner longitudinal timber that runs from stem to stern at the chine.

Cleat A wood or metal fitting with two projecting horns, fastened to some part of the boat, to which a line is belayed.

Clenched nail A nail whose point has been bent back into the wood; most often used in lapstrake planking.

Clew The lower after corner of a sail, where the foot meets the leech.

Clinker-built A hull with lapstrake planking is said to be clinker-built; also called clench-built.

Clipper bow A bow whose stem reverses direction to form a concave curve, and projects outboard.

Club A small spar laced to the foot of a sail; sometimes used on the after edge of a fore-and-aft sail, as on a log canoe.

Coaming A raised framing around deck openings such as hatches or cockpits, to keep water out.

Counter The lower portion of the stern that extends above and over the water.

Covering board The wide, outermost, fore-and-aft plank on either side of the deck.

Crab A metal pedestal secured on deck abaft the mast; used as a gooseneck fitting on catboats.

Cringle A metal ring, grommet or piece of rope set in the corners or on the edges of a sail and used for fastening the sail to spars or running rigging.

Crosscut sail A sail whose seams run at right angles to the leech.

Crosstrees A spreader through which the masthead shrouds are led.

Cutwater The forward edge of a boat's stem; also describes a false stem.

Deadeye A thick, hardwood disk usually pierced with three holes through which lanyards are rove; used as a block to connect shrouds and chain plates.

Deadrise The angle at which the bottom rises from where it joins the keel to the turn of the bilge, or chine.

Deadwood The solid timbering in the below-water sections of the bow or stern; most commonly used to build up a skeg in the after end.

Diagonals In the lines plan of a round-bottomed boat, the set of lines corresponding to slices made at an angle down from the center line to the outside of the hull; used to check sections' accuracy.

Double planking A planking method in which two staggered layers of smooth fore-and-aft strakes make up the hull.

Dutchman A wooden plug used to fill in a cavity in a hull member.

Entry The forebody of a hull where it enters the water.

Eyesplice A permanent loop made at a rope's end by weaving unlaid strands into the standing part of the line.

Fair In lofting, to correct a hull's lines with the use of a batten, making them even and regular.

Fairlead An eye or block that guides a line in a desired direction.

Fall The hauling end or section of a line in a tackle; used in the plural, a synonym for tackle.

Fall off A boat is said to fall off when its head moves away from the direction of the wind.

False stem A separate timber that attaches to an inner stem covering the ends of the side planking; also called a cutwater.

Fisherman's staysail A quadrilateral sail set between the foremast and mainmast of a schooner.

Flare Outward spread and upward curve of the topsides as they rise from the waterline, most noticeable in the bow.

Floor timbers Athwartships timbers that attach to keel and frame heels and serve to unify the backbone and framing as well as strengthen the lowermost strakes.

Flying A term describing a sail not bent to any spar or stay and controlled by its halyard, tack line and sheet.

Foot The bottom edge of a sail.

Forefoot The forward portion of a boat where the stem meets the keel.

Futtocks Individual timbers that are fastened together to make up a frame.

Gaff A spar to support and spread the head of a sail of four generally unequal sides. A sail so rigged is said to be gaff-headed.

Garboard The plank, or strake, next to the keel.

Gollywobbler On a schooner, a jumbo fisherman's staysail.

Gooseneck The fitting that connects the boom to the mast and allows the boom to swing laterally and vertically.

Gripe A curved timber used to join the keel to the stem.

Grommet A small eyelet in a sail through which a lacing or a roband passes.

Gunwale The top edge of a boat's side (pronounced GUN-nel).

Half-breadth view In a lines plan, the view of the hull as seen from above.

Hanging knee A wooden brace that fastens to the hull's side and supports deck beams or decking.

Head The forward part of a boat, including the bow and adjacent areas; the uppermost corner of a triangular sail; a seagoing toilet.

Head ledges Vertical timbers at either end of a centerboard case to which the case's planks fasten.

Heave to The general term for positioning the boat at an angle to the wind and sea that will permit it to ride as comfortably as possible, making little or no headway. Generally, a sailboat is hove to with her head about 60° off the wind.

Hogging piece See Keel batten.

Horn timber A timber that runs from the stern post to the transom along the center line and supports the overhang in the stern of a boat with a counter.

Jaws A wooden, U-shaped fitting that holds the gaff or the boom to the mast.

Jewel block A small single block.

Keel batten In small boats, a fore-and-aft timber secured atop the keel to provide a surface to which the garboard strakes can be fastened; also called a hogging piece.

Keelson In large vessels, an inner fore-and-aft timber used to strengthen the hull longitudinally; usually bolted on top of the keel.

King plank A wide deck plank that runs along the center line.

Knee A triangular-shaped piece of wood used to strengthen the connection between two structural members.

Knightheads Vertical timbers on either side of the stem that add strength to the bowsprit and provide additional backing to the planking just abaft the stem.

Lanyard A line used for making anything fast; also, the rope that reeves through deadeyes.

Lapstrake planking A planking method in which the strakes overlap one another.

Lateen A triangular mainsail extended fore and aft of a short mast at roughly a 45° angle by means of a long yard.

Lay The direction in which the strands of a line are twisted, usually right-handed or clockwise.

Lazy jacks Light lines running from mast to boom on either side of the sail; used to contain the sail as it is lowered.

Leech The after edge of a fore-and-aft sail.

Lignum vitae A dense, tropical hardwood commonly used in the manufacture of blocks, deadeyes and other heavy-stress marine fittings.

Limber holes Notches cut into a boat's frames or floor timbers near the keel to allow bilge water to run to the lowest point in the hull.

Lines plan A set of drawings showing the shape of a hull as delineated by its sections, buttocks, waterlines and diagonals.

Load waterline In a lines plan, the line that indicates the level at which the hull will meet the surface of the water when floating upright with its designed load on board.

Loft To scale up and draw a lines plan to actual size on a large floor. The final drawing is called the lofting.

Loose-footed A term used to describe a boomless sail.

Luff The leading edge of a fore-and-aft sail; also, the fluttering of a sail when the boat is pointed too close to the wind or the sail is let out too far.

Lug A quadrilateral sail bent to a long yard that hangs obliquely from a short mast.

Marline Two-stranded nautical twine.

Mast hoop A ring, usually of wood, by which the luff of a sail is held to the mast.

Mast step A socket in which the heel, or bottom, of a mast is stepped.

Molds Wooden sectional patterns, set on stations across the keel, around which planks are bent to obtain the precise shape of a boat.

Offsets A table of coordinates that provide the full-scale measurements needed to loft a lines plan.

Parcel To wind strips of canvas tightly around the lay of a rope before serving. The canvas thus used is called parceling.

Parrel line A line attached to the forward ends of a gaff's jaws that holds the gaff to the mast. The line is often strung with lignum vitae beads called parrel beads.

Partners Reinforcing timbers, on the underside of the deck, that form a frame to support through-deck structures such as masts, capstans or Samson posts.

Peak The upper, outer corner of a gaff-headed sail.

Pin rail A rail, generally mounted at the base of a mast, and fitted with sturdy pins for belaying running rigging.

Profile In a lines plan, the view of the hull as seen from the side; also called the elevation or sheer plan.

Purchase A tackle, usually permanently rigged; also, the mechanical advantage gained by using a tackle.

Quarter knee A horizontal knee connecting the boat's side with the transom.

Rabbet In a boat, a V-shaped groove cut into the backbone, and into which the planking fits.

Rabbet line A line representing the outer edge of a rabbet.

Rake As a noun, the inclination from the perpendicular—usually aft in the case of masts.

Reef To reduce sail area without removing the sail entirely.

Reefing comb A piece of hardwood fixed to the outer end of a boom through which a series of holes have been bored to provide fairleads for reef pendants.

Reefing pendant A short rope rove through a cringle at either end of a row of reef points, whose purpose is to secure a reefed sail atop the boom.

Reef points Short lines, attached to the body of a sail and ranged in one or more rows, which serve as tie-downs when sail must be reduced.

Reeve To pass the end of a line through a hole or opening, as through a block or a fairlead.

Ribbands In boatbuilding, fore-and-aft wood strips temporarily attached to the molds to hold the frames in place as they are bent or placed in the hull.

Riding turns A second layer of turns wrapped over a seizing or whipping; also known as riders.

Riser A fore-and-aft strip fastened on the

inside of frames to support the ends of thwarts.

Robands Short light lines used to attach a sail to a bending jackstay or mast hoops.

Rocker A convex, fore-and-aft curvature in the keel or bottom of a hull.

Round up To bring the boat's head to the wind; also, the haul up slack in a tackle.

Rove A copper washer over which the point of a copper nail has been splayed; also, the past tense of the verb to reeve.

Rub rail See Sheer guard.

Samson post A single bitt at the bow of a boat.

Scandalize To reduce sail in an unusual manner, as by removing the sprit on a spritsail.

Scantlings The dimensions of all structural parts such as frames, planks and fastenings of a boat; commonly recorded on a boat's construction plan.

Scarph A lapped joint used to make one continuous piece out of two timbers.

Scull To swing an oar or tiller back and forth through the water off the stern of a boat to move the boat forward.

Sections In a lines plan, the contour lines that represent athwartships slices through the hull's surface.

Seize To bind two lines together or bind a line to another object.

Sennit Braided cordage made from untarred marline, rope yarns or spun yarn and plaited by hand.

Serve To wind cord, yard or marline tightly around a line, keeping the turns close together; used around parceling to protect it from water damage.

Shaft log A timber that forms part of a wood boat's keel or deadwood section, and which is bored lengthwise to take a propeller shaft.

Sheave The grooved wheel in a block, or in a masthead fitting or elsewhere, over which a rope runs (pronounced SHIV).

Sheer clamp A fore-and-aft timber, fastened over the inboard side of the frames, that runs along or just below the hull's sheer line; often simply called clamp.

Sheer guard A fender rail attached to the outside of the hull along the sheer line; also called a rub rail.

Sheer line The fore-and-aft curve of the hull at deck level from stem to stern.

Sheer strake The uppermost planking strip or strake, so called because its top edge defines the vessel's sheer; often of a heavier, stronger wood as it provides extra longitudinal bracing.

Shrouds Ropes or wires led from the mast to chain plates at deck level on either side of the mast to keep it vertical.

Shutter The final strake or plank inserted during the planking of the hull; it is usually located roughly midway between the sheer and garboard strakes.

Snotter A short length of line, made fast around the mast of a sprit-rigged boat, that holds the lower end of the sprit in position.

Spring stay A horizontal stay running between two mastheads of a schooner.

Sprit A light spar that crosses a fore-and-aft sail, usually on the diagonal, to hold the peak aloft.

Stations In lines plans and loftings, points marked off on the base line that correspond with the sections.

Stem The principal framing member of the bow to which the planking is fastened; also, the forwardmost part of the bow.

Stern post The upright timber joined to the after end of the keel; the post on which the rudder is usually mounted.

Stern sheets In a small boat, the aft thwart seat and attached side seats, that run to the transom.

Stopwater A softwood dowel driven into the joints between backbone timbers to prevent water from leaking into the hull along the seam.

Strake A strip of planking running the length of the hull.

Strip building A planking method in which strips of wood are edge-fastened together to form the hull.

Strongback A heavy reinforcing timber that runs athwartships and rests on top of the keel, as in the skipjack.

Tack To alter a boat's course through the eye of the wind; also, the lower forward corner of a sail.

Tackle An arrangement of lines rove through blocks to provide mechanical advantage for hoisting or hauling (pronounced TAY-kel).

Thole pins Wood or metal pins fitted into a rowboat's gunwales to serve the same purpose as oarlocks.

Throat The forward or mast end of a gaff, usually fitted with jaws; also, the adjacent corner of the sail.

Thumb cleat A one-horned cleat fixed to a mast or other spar to prevent a line such as a snotter from slipping its position.

Tie rod A metal bolt or threaded rod used for structural reinforcement, as between the cockpit carlin and the hull side.

Toe rail A narrow wooden strip running along the outer edge of the deck to check slippery footing.

Tongue A block of wood, mounted on a pivot bolt between the gaff jaws, and between the gaff and the mast, to facilitate the gaff's movement up and down the mast.

Topmast A mast placed above a lower mast and overlapping it on the forward side for several feet.

Topping lift A line that runs from the masthead to the end of the boom to help take the weight of the boom; also used to adjust the angle of the boom.

Topsail A sail set on a topmast.

Trailboards A pair of ornamental boards running between the bowsprit and the bows, which sometimes flank a figurehead.

Trap A form over which steamed frames may be bent prior to fitting them into the hull.

Traveler A bar or track secured athwartships on a deck or cabin top so that the sheet of a sail, attached to the traveler by a block and slide, can move back and forth.

Treenail A wooden pin, usually of locust, driven through a snug hole bored in adjoining timbers so as to fasten them together. A small wedge is driven into each end to lodge the treenail firmly in place (pronounced TRUN-nel).

Tricing line A line that draws up a sail; used to reduce sail by raising its foot.

Turn of the bilge In a round-bottomed boat, the curve where the bottom meets the topsides.

Turnbuckle A fastening that connects the standing rigging to the chain plates and is used to adjust the tension in the standing rigging.

Waterlines In a lines plan, the contour lines that represent horizontal, lengthwise slices of the hull's surface, parallel with its load waterline.

Weather helm The tendency of a sailboat to head up toward the wind.

Whip To wrap something for protection, usually with cord or line.

Worm To wind tarred rope or yarn spirally around and between the strands of a rope before parceling. The material thus used is called worming.

Yoke The crosspiece fitted on the rudderhead of a small boat and used for steering where a tiller would be impractical. A pair of lines leading from the ends of the yoke control the rudder.

Acknowledgments

The index was prepared by Anita R. Beckerman. The editors also wish to thank the following: E. L. Boutilier, Medomak, Maine; Vince Callahan, Weirs Beach, New Hampshire; J. Revell Carr, Mystic Seaport, Inc., Mystic, Connecticut; Dr. William Earle Geoghegan, Division of Transportation, Smithsonian Institution, Washington, D.C.; Dr. Peter J. Guthorn, Neptune City, New Jersey; Howard Hallas, Secretary-Treasurer, Chris-Craft Antique Boat Club, Highlands, North Carolina; A. Sidney DeW. Herreshoff, Bristol, Rhode Island; Sohei Hohri, Librarian,

New York Yacht Club, New York, New York; Jim Irwin, Irwin Marine, Lakeport, New Hampshire; Patricia E. Kelly, Mystic Seaport, Inc., Mystic, Connecticut; Mr. and Mrs. Robert L. Kelly, Little Silver, New Jersey; John Leavens, Chilmark, Massachusetts; Newell McLain, Thomaston, Maine; Kenneth E. Mahler, Mystic Seaport, Inc., Mystic, Connecticut; Mr. and Mrs. John H. Malmquist, Red Bank, New Jersey; Mrs. M. C. Marshall Jr., Secretary, Chesapeake Bay Log Sailing Canoe Association, St. Michaels, Maryland; Capt. and Mrs. W. S. Morrow III, East Sandwich,

Massachusetts; Ray Nelson, *Antique Boating*, Cleverdale, New York; Mr. and Mrs. John B. Nichols, New Rochelle, New York; Jarvis Newman, Southwest Harbor, Maine; Ralph Stanley, Southwest Harbor, Maine; Mary Anne Stets, Mystic Seaport, Inc., Mystic, Connecticut; Vance Strausburg, St. Michaels, Maryland; Bob Valpey, Vintage Antique Boat and Motorcar Co., Holderness, New Hampshire; Tom Willis, Vessel Administration & Documentation, Rockland, Maine.

Picture Credits

Credits for illustrations from left to right are separated by semicolons; from top to bottom by dashes. Some elements in the lines and construction plans contained in this book have been rearranged or omitted for clarity or to accommodate space limitations. None of the plans should be used for construction purposes. All plans from Howard I. Chapelle's American Small Sailing Craft and Boatbuilding are used with the permission of W. W. Norton & Company, Inc., copyrights 1951 and 1969 respectively, and are courtesy the Smithsonian Institution.

Cover—Stephen Green-Armytage. 6,7 —Bob Grieser. 9—Official Mystic Seaport photo by Kenneth E. Mahler. 12—Dennis L. Crow. 14—Reynolds-Shafer Studios —Stuart Gannes. 15—Stephen Green-Armytage. 16,17—Al Freni (2); Peter Barlow. 18—Wendy Rieder. 19—Peter Barlow —Al Freni (2); Peter Barlow. 20,21—Stephen Green-Armytage except top right Clyde H. Smith. 22,23—Sue Cummings; Bill Schill. 24—Jack Murphy. 25—Stephen Green-Armytage. 26—Chris Caswell —Diane Beeston. 27,28,29—Diane Beeston. 30—Courtesy Vineyard Yachts, Inc. 31—David Q. Scott courtesy Peter Van Dine, Inc. 32,33—Stephen Green-Armytage courtesy Jarvis Newman; Norman Fortier courtesy Marshall Marine—Ted Heidenreich Jr. courtesy Doughdish, Inc.; courtesy Tenants Harbor Boat Works. 34—Courtesy Penobscot Boat Works —courtesy Peter Van Dine. 35—Courtesy Golden Era Boats—courtesy Classic Boat Builders. 36,37—Photo of model by Robert Perron courtesy Mystic Seaport, Inc. Background lines drawings by Fred Wolff after drawings by Robert A. Pittaway

based on material by E. I. Schock, courtesy Mystic Seaport, Inc. and background construction plan drawings by R. C. Allyn, courtesy Mystic Seaport, Inc. 38—Drawings by Whitman Studio, Inc. after lines plans by Robert A. Pittaway based on material by E. I. Schock, courtesy Mystic Seaport, Inc. 39,40,41—Drawings by Fred Wolff after lines plans by Robert A. Pittaway based on material by E. I. Schock, courtesy Mystic Seaport, Inc. 42,43 —Drawings by Fred Wolff. Lofting after lines plans by Robert A. Pittaway based on material by E. I. Schock, courtesy Mystic Seaport, Inc. 44—Drawing by Dale Gustafson after lines plans by Robert A. Pittaway based on material by E. I. Schock and drawings by R. C. Allyn, courtesy Mystic Seaport, Inc.—drawings by R. C. Allyn, courtesy Mystic Seaport, Inc. 45,46,47 —Drawings by Dale Gustafson after lines plans by Robert A. Pittaway based on material by E. I. Schock and drawings by R. C. Allyn, courtesy Mystic Seaport, Inc. 48,49—Top drawing by Whitman Studio, Inc. after construction plans by Howard I. Chapelle in *American Small Sailing Craft* —all bottom drawings by Fred Wolff. Noank skiff drawings after plans courtesy Mystic Seaport, Inc., No Mans Land and Connecticut River drag boat plans adapted from *American Small Sailing Craft* by Howard I. Chapelle, Fisherman's launch and Peapod adapted from *Boatbuilding* by Howard I. Chapelle, Whitehall after plans by Robert A. Pittaway courtesy Mystic Seaport, Inc. 50 through 53—Drawings by Dale Gustafson. 54,55—Drawings by Whitman Studio, Inc. 56,57—Drawings by Dale Gustafson except top left plans adapted from *American Small Sailing Craft* by Howard I. Chapelle. 58,59

—Drawings by Dale Gustafson except top left plans adapted from *American Small Sailing Craft* by Howard I. Chapelle. 60,61 —Drawings at right and bottom by Dale Gustafson based on plans in top left box by Howard I. Chapelle from *American Small Sailing Craft*. 62—Bottom drawing by Dale Gustafson based on plans at top drawn by Robert A. Pittaway, courtesy Mystic Seaport, Inc. 63—Drawings by Dale Gustafson based on plans on page 62. 64—Bottom drawing by Dale Gustafson based on top plans by Howard I. Chapelle from *American Small Sailing Craft*. 65—Drawing by Fred Wolff adapted from plans by Howard I. Chapelle in *Fishing Boats of the World*, Vol. 1, © 1955 Food and Agriculture Organization of the United Nations—drawing by Dale Gustafson based on plan at top. 66,67—Courtesy A. Sidney DeW. Herreshoff. 68,69—Courtesy Halsey Herreshoff—Charles Sylvester courtesy A. Sidney DeW. Herreshoff; courtesy A. Sidney DeW. Herreshoff. 70,71—Courtesy A. Sidney DeW. Herreshoff; Morris Rosenfeld courtesy A. Sidney DeW. Herreshoff. 72,73—Paul Darling; courtesy A. Sidney DeW. Herreshoff —Paul Darling. 74,75—Courtesy A. Sidney DeW. Herreshoff. 76,77—Morris Rosenfeld. 78—Jarvis Newman. 80—Courtesy Newell McLain—map by Joe Argenziano. 81—Courtesy Percy Torrey—courtesy C. Peter Chesney. 82,83—Jarvis Newman —drawings by Adolph Brotman. 84 —Drawings by Fred Wolff based on original drawings by Ralph Stanley. 86 —Stephen Green-Armytage. 88 through 91—Drawings by Adolph Brotman. 92 —Jarvis Newman. 93—Jarvis Newman —Reese Hassig. 94,95—Stephen Green-Armytage. 96—Drawing by Whitman Studio, Inc.—Stephen Green-Armytage. 98,99—Stephen Green-Armytage. 100 through 119—Dan Budnik. 120,121—Al Freni. 122—Clyde H. Smith—Stephen Green-Armytage. 123—Stephen· Green-Armytage. 124,125—Stephen Green-Armytage; Dan Budnik—Dan Budnik (2); Stephen Green-Armytage. 126,127—Dan Budnik. 128—Stuart Gannes. 130—Drawings by Dale Gustafson. 131—Drawings by Dale Gustafson except top right drawings by Fred Wolff (2). 132—Drawings by Fred Wolff except top right drawing by Peter McGinn. 133—Drawings by Peter Mc-Ginn except top right drawings by Fred Wolff. 134,135—Drawings by John Sagan. 136—Drawing by Dale Gustafson. 137—Drawings by Dale Gustafson—drawings by Whitman Studio, Inc. (2). 138—Drawing by Dale Gustafson. 139—Drawings by Whitman Studio, Inc. 140—Drawings by Fred Wolff. 141—Drawings by Adolph Brotman. 142 through 145—Drawings by Whitman Studio, Inc. 146—Drawing by Dale Gustafson. 147—Drawings by Whitman Studio, Inc. 148, 149—Drawings by Roger Metcalf. 150—Drawing by Dale Gustafson. 151—Drawing by Adolph Brotman—drawing by Whitman Studio, Inc. 152—Drawing by Whitman Studio, Inc. 153—Drawings by Whitman Studio, Inc.—Morris Rosenfeld. 154—Drawings by Whitman Studio, Inc. 155—Drawings by Roger Metcalf. 157 through 165—Bob Grieser.

Index
Page numbers in italics indicate an illustration of the subject mentioned.